T0344415

ALDO GALLI

THE POLLAIUOLO

5 CONTINENTS

PAGE 2
Late-fifteenth-century unknown sculptor, *Funerary Monument of Antonio and Piero del Pollaiuolo*, Rome, San Pietro in Vincoli.

EDITORIAL COORDINATOR
Paola Gallerani

TRANSLATION
Susan Wise

EDITING
Andrew Ellis

ICONOGRAPHIC RESEARCH
Alessandra Montini

CONSULTANT ART DIRECTOR
Orna Frommer-Dawson

GRAPHIC DESIGN
John and Orna Designs, London

LAYOUT
Virginia Maccagno

COLOUR SEPARATION
Cross Media Network srl (Milan)

PRINTED JUNE 2005
by Conti Tipocolor, Calenzano (Florence)

© 2005 – 5 Continents Editions srl, Milan
info@5continentseditions.com
ISBN 88-7439-130-7

PRINTED IN ITALY

CONTENTS

A BLURRED IMAGE

Today Antonio del Pollaiuolo's name instantly brings to mind his most famous paintings, all prized icons in the finest canonical Florentine Renaissance style: the great London altarpiece, with its brawny archers dancing around the stake to which pl. 23 Saint Sebastian is tied; the tousled *Hercules* of the two small panels in the Uffizi in pls. 16, 17 Florence; the three dandy-saints preening in the altarpiece of the Cardinal of pl. 9 Portugal, also in the Uffizi; or the female portrait in sharp profile in the Museo Poldi pl. 15 Pezzoli in Milan, adopted as the museum's logo. Piero's name means a great deal less since a widespread established interpretative tradition reduced him to playing second fiddle to his older brother, as though he were but an obscure workshop assistant. For instance, the entry for the Pollaiuolo in the popular *Garzantina Arte* encyclopaedia states no less that: "critics […] agree in identifying Piero's presence where the quality is poorer, the sign least incisive and sharp, the colour muddier". This sharing of responsibility between the two brothers should probably be re-examined, particularly as a fair number of the panels that drew so much enthusiasm from Bernard Berenson and his early twentieth-century admirers actually turn out to be by Piero, although Antonio retains the supremacy that even his contemporaries had already acknowledged. But let us proceed in order.

The striking predilection for painting, so obvious in the studies that between the nineteenth and twentieth centuries laid the foundations of modern art history (from Cavalcaselle to Berenson to Longhi), undoubtedly assigned to paintings a primary role within a highly articulated corpus like the one ascribed to the Pollaiuolo brothers, that also included monumental and collector bronzes, goldsmithery, ceramics, enamels, etchings, and embroideries. Yet Antonio del Pollaiuolo, as he declared in the epitaph he dictated for his tomb, felt his true claim to fame lay in the monumental pls. 28, 31 bronzes he mounted in the Vatican for the mortal remains of Sixtus IV and Innocent VIII, at a time when he considered he had reached the height and conclusion of an extraordinary career. And precisely it was as caster and goldsmith that his contemporaries praised him, distinguishing him from younger Piero, who was mentioned if anything as a painter—skilled to be sure, but not of his brother's stature. We need but take a look at the testimonies of those who knew them to grasp immediately how much the perception in fifteenth-century Italy of the two enterprising sons of Jacopo Benci, who sold poultry in the Mercato Vecchio of Florence, differed from the modern one. Antonio Filarete, for instance, who in his *Trattato d'architettura* (*Treatise on Architecture*) devised a city for the dukes of Milan— more mythical than ideal—could easily see the elder of the two Pollaiuolo as one of the goldsmiths to be employed on the cathedral high altar, upon which he imagined a gold and enamel altarpiece under a gilt bronze canopy "adorned with various carvings and figures". In Urbino twenty years later Giovanni Santi was rather vague in calling the brothers "such great draughtsmen" (*Cronaca rimata*, Book XXII), but elsewhere he lauds in uneven yet ardent rhymes the gilt helmet that in 1473 the Florentines had offered to Federico da Montefeltro, conqueror of Volterra, and that Antonio had crowned with a statuette of "Hercules invincible who, clenching his teeth, / underfoot like a rebellious beast, / held a griffin chained by the neck, / that used to be the arms of ancient Volterra, / and plumed of its primaries, / lay humbled at its victor's feet / with wounds all over its body " (Book XIII). The Latin verses of the Florentine Ugolino Verino are more professional, and when celebrating the brothers on several occasions he does not fail to emphasise Antonio's primacy as a sculptor: "Nec Pulli fratres ornandi laude minore: clarior at fuso longe est Antonius aere" (The Pollaiuolo brothers are not to be praised less: but by far the most illustrious is Antonio for his cast bronzes; *De illustratione urbis Florentiae*). Then at the end of the century, in Rome, in at least five tercets of his *Antiquarie prospetiche romane*, the mysterious painter-poet who had himself called "Prospectivo Melanese", composed

pl. 28   garbled yet resounding and visionary praise of the Funerary Monument to Sixtus IV, the only modern work in the city that was a match for the antique.

Then, leaving aside the humanists' paganising and somewhat sporadic celebrations, if we turn to the art literature of the early sixteenth century the different skills of the two brothers are clearly defined. For Francesco Albertini writing in 1510 (barely twelve years after Antonio's death) as well as for the *Libro di Antonio Billi* and the manuscript of the writer known as the Anonimo Magliabechiano, the elder Pollaiuolo is a "goldsmith of the greatest conception [...] [who] works niello and the burin superbly". His catalogue includes parts of the silver altar with the *Stories of Saint John*

pl. 8   for the Florentine baptistery, the designs provided to the embroiderers of the
pl. 6   paraments also for the baptistery, the famous etching, signed, with the *Battle of the Ten*
pls. 28, 31   *Nudes* and the two papal tombs. On the other hand, Piero, a "Florentine painter", is
pl. 23   the author of the *Martyrdom of Saint Sebastian* then at the Santissima Annunziata and now in London; a colossal frescoed *Saint Christopher* on the facade of the church
pls. 12-14   (destroyed) of San Miniato fra le Torri; six figures of the *Virtues* painted for the

Tribunale di Mercanzia (Guild of Merchants), the panel in memory of the Cardinal of pl. 10
Portugal in San Miniato al Monte; and the canvas with *Saint Antoninus adoring the* pl. 26
Crucifix on the saint's tomb at San Marco. Two distinct personalities and catalogues, as
is punctually confirmed as well by the existence—attested by the two brothers' fiscal
declarations and other contemporary evidence—of two separate workshops, one,
a goldsmith's, in Via Vacchereccia, next to Piazza della Signoria, and the other, a
painter's, in Piazza degli Agli, not far from the baptistery.

VASARI'S LIVES

The first to create confusion was Giorgio Vasari. Straight away the writer from Arezzo
saw the opportunity to use the figure of Antonio, born the humble son of a poulterer
and raised to official artist at the papal courts and a man of great wealth, to build an
exemplary biography laden with broader ideological implications, overlooking when
necessary the exact circumstances of the artist's historical life. In Vasari's tale Antonio's
irresistible social promotion actually matches a parallel evolution: from the more
mechanical aspects of art to the more elect, intellectual ones, according to a rigid
hierarchy relative to the degree of nobility of the various disciplines. While such a
view would have been unthinkable in the city of Lorenzo il Magnifico, it seemed
entirely plausible to the readers of the *Lives* in mid-sixteenth-century ducal Florence.
Hence a sublimation which from goldsmithery (a technique that for Vasari was no
more than diligent craftsmanship) rose to bronze sculpture, and thence to the very
noble art of painting, which could far better insure the artist's lasting fame. Piero did
not fit into this literary project, so we have the Pollaiuolo brothers merged in a single
biography (whereas the records prior to Vasari had always distinguished the
information regarding each of them), with just one protagonist, Antonio, while the
younger brother was reduced to the merely functional role of leading his elder to
painting. Indeed, in striving to somehow reconcile the indications of the sources with
his more complicated narrative requirements, Vasari imagined young Antonio
studying goldsmithery with Ghiberti, and Piero an apprentice painter with Andrea del
Castagno. However, after his first successes in working in silver and enamel, Antonio
realized that goldwork did not "give long life to the toils of its creators", so decided to
change professions "out of the desire to be longer remembered". A brisk training
course with his brother and a few paintings executed with him soon made Antonio an
excellent painter, far superior to Piero, who at this point disappeared, allowing Vasari
to concentrate everything on his hero, who was thus awarded the most famous panels,
first of all the *Saint Sebastian* for the Annunziata. To make his reconstruction more pl. 23
creditable, Vasari may even have gone so far as to commit a conscious omission: on the

high altar of the Augustinians' church at San Gimignano loomed (and still looms
pl. 24 today) a large altarpiece with the *Coronation of the Virgin*, signed and dated in very
large letters "PIERO DEL POLLAIUOLO FIORENTINO 1483". Vasari had to be familiar with
it, since in the *Life* of Benozzo Gozzoli he described with sincere praise the latter's
frescoes that cover the walls surrounding it. The biographer-painter's expert eye could
not have missed how similar that panel was in composition, figures, and technique, to
the paintings he had placed at the heart of Antonio's catalogue. So he chose to simply
overlook the existence of the awkward document.

For almost three centuries Vasari's authority was unchallenged and the version of the
facts proposed in that twin biography was believed by everyone until investigations in
the archives finally began to reveal a quite different reality to nineteenth-century
researchers.

Among the first to become aware of it were Giovan Battista Cavalcaselle and Joseph
Crowe who, in the classic *New History of Painting in Italy* (1864–66), rightly turned to
a distribution of the Pollaiuolo brothers' skills more in line with the testimonies
preceding Vasari. Nonetheless, the hierarchies of values among the various artistic
techniques set up in the sixteenth century still influenced historians' judgements. A
mere goldsmith Antonio—without the famous paintings that were the pride of the
greatest galleries in Europe—could not satisfy the myth of the champion of the
Florentine Renaissance: Bernard Berenson in the early twentieth century forcefully
claimed those paintings as belonging to the greatest of the two Pollaiuolo, entirely to
the detriment of the other, permanently recorded as Antonio's insignificant accessory.
And since in those years Berenson's power of persuasion was almost equal to the
influence of Vasari's opinions over the sixteenth and seventeenth centuries, his
reconstruction of the relationship between the two brothers was soon so crystallised
into dogma, that most of the Pollaiuolo monographs written in the last century are
devoted to Antonio alone, although paintings are always given the lion's share. It is
not until recently that going back to reflect on references preceding Vasari's biography,
we have cautiously begun to make some adjustments, although Piero has not yet
recovered a clear, historically plausible physiognomy.

So should all the sculptures be given back to Antonio and all the paintings to Piero? It
is not as simple as that. If it is highly probable that the younger Pollaiuolo never
touched a chisel nor took to casting, on the other hand Antonio did occasionally
work with the paintbrush. He himself was the one to tell us so, first, in that list of
his skills that he slipped into the signatures of the two pontifical tombs ("Antonio
Pollaiuolo, famous in gold, silver, bronze and painting"), and second, in a letter in
1494, by then an old man, he wrote to Gentil Virginio Orsini, duke of Bracciano, in

which he recalled the three large canvases with the *Labours of Hercules* painted in his youth for the Palazzo Medici in Florence. A pictorial production that must in any case have been quite limited and indeed concentrated in the early stages of his career, since already his contemporaries, as we have seen, did not mention it and apparently sixteenth-century historiographers had entirely forgotten it. Imagining it today is not an easy task since the Medici paintings have been lost for centuries and there are no paintings signed by Antonio. To identify his share among the many "Pollaiuolesque" pictures, we must focus on the ones that are farthest removed from the rich shimmering painterly styling—explicitly Netherlandish in inspiration, mindful of the orient of pearls, the texture of silks and velvets, the sheen of polished marbles—that is the most special characteristic of the *Coronation of the Virgin* signed by Piero at San   pl. 24 Gimignano, and also on the other paintings that pre-Vasari sources attributed to the younger Pollaiuolo. So now that the confused historiographical issue has been clarified, the time has come to take a close look at the images.

ANTONIO DEL POLLAIUOLO, GOLDSMITH AND MASTER DRAUGHTSMAN

Antonio was born in Florence in late 1431 or early 1432, the firstborn of six brothers. We have no accurate information about his training that some sixteenth-century records consider to have been with Lorenzo Ghiberti on the yard of the Porta del Paradiso. The "connoisseurs" of Vasari's generation, who liked to identify the hand of several collaborators in those teeming gilded leaves, even pointed out the beginner Antonio's personal contribution: a quail pecking about amidst the chaff at about mid-height of the left door jamb. Although the notion enjoyed some credit even in recent times, it is advisable to be somewhat cautious as regards the over-confident connoisseurship in which the sixteenth century indulged in this field. Ghiberti's two doors, on which scores of goldsmiths, sculptors and painters, great or small, had indeed spent more or less extended periods of apprenticeship, were steeped in a mythical aura by the artists of the Florence of a hundred years later. There was not a single fifteenth-century master who was not believed to have modelled a small head or given the finishing touch, precisely, to some sort of beast of those luxuriant bronze works. In the pages of the Anonimo Magliabechiano, Giorgio Vasari, and Baccio Bandinelli, the list of those who worked on the doors became more and more crowded and less and less creditable from the point of view of chronology as well as style: Niccolò Lamberti and the two Rossellino, Parri Spinelli and Desiderio da Settignano, Filarete and Verrocchio, and even Lorenzo's eternal rival Filippo Brunelleschi. Although the dates do not prevent Antonio from having had that experience (Ghiberti died in 1455), the fact remains that even in Pollaiuolo's earliest works there is not a hint of Ghiberti's wavy refinements, faultless falcate garments, nor of the cautiously classicising grace associated with his heads. We can follow a far more promising track to explain Antonio's apprenticeship. It leads to the vast map of family-run Florentine goldsmith workshops, presently almost forgotten, with which Antonio was apparently connected at the outset of his career and over the years associated in collaborations and partnerships aimed at insuring the utmost efficiency to his undertakings. At the time of Pollaiuolo's formation, the most outstanding *bottega* of all was the Finiguerra's, where Maso (1426–64), scarcely older than Antonio, was the star, a most renowned goldsmith in those days, although his real artistic identity still eludes us. The plaques in nielloed silver were among the most admired items Maso created, small, precious plates upon which he was able to compose stories with dozens of figures, samples of the extraordinary skill in draughtsmanship that was associated with his fame. Along with these subtle, elaborate carved works on metal (several examples conserved in the Museo del Bargello express a marked predilection for the formal world of Filippo Lippi), we have the many drawings that, after lengthy debate, have unanimously been attributed to Finiguerra, and are the necessary premise for the development of Antonio del Pollaiuolo's graphic style. These are figures of workshop youths caught in entirely informal attitudes, busy drawing or asleep on the bench or posing as Davids or Saint Sebastians, but always individualised by a sharp accurate sign that creates the form simply by means of an outline, at the most enhanced with some slight watercolour modelling. This special linear virtuosity that Pollaiuolo would carry to the utmost after breaking free from Maso's slightly dry, over-careful line makes the Finiguerra workshop the ideal place for his formation.

Works and documents allow to follow Antonio's lucky star beginning in 1457. While he did not yet have his own workshop, his name must already have possessed some prestige, since he received a commission as important as the Silver Cross for the altar of the baptistery in Florence, the acme of Renaissance silverwork, miraculously survived. Antonio was called to execute the lower half, that is, the foot and base of the monumental furnishing—two and a half metres high—while another master, Betto Betti, was to provide the cross itself. Each of them received payment for his share in 1459 from the Arte di Calimala (the wool and textile guild) that was in charge of the decoration and furnishings of the baptistery, where the grandiose silverwork would be solemnly exhibited in the coming centuries on the occasion of the feast day of Saint John, Florence's patron saint. Wonderfully rich, intricate and sumptuous yet at the same time precise, the cross reflects a significant architectonic ambition in Pollaiuolo's base; it rests on a wide foot with a star-shaped profile, strewn with enamel figurations and the Calamala arms. Two harpies cling to it, each gracefully supporting on their lush curly locks a statuette of a worshipping angel. Other angels and the figure of the Baptist, repeated twice, occupy the niches of the base upon whose imbricated small dome Betto Betti's part soars, with the Christ nailed to a cross dazzling with

pl. 1

pl. 2

enamels, and the statues of the mourners flanking him upheld by ample scrolls. The polychrome inlays have almost all disappeared. While this reduces the visual gorgeousness of the ensemble, it allows us to discover the wonderful subtlety of the underlying figures on the silver sheet. For instance the *Baptism of Christ*, within the limited space of the plaque, describes the joints of the Baptist's hands and feet, Christ's chest with its jutting sternum, the countless folds of the tunics, and even the water poured out of the Precursor's cup and veiling Christ's body. pl. 4

Even before the cross was completed, Antonio received new commissions and they were always sacred goldwork: two pyxes for the cathedral, and a thurible for the Vallombrosan church of San Pancrazio. They must have given great satisfaction since shortly afterward, on 3 January 1461, the abbot of that convent commissioned him together with the less well-known Piero Sali, "companions in a goldsmith workshop", for a more challenging silver reliquary to shelter the arm of the titular saint, a gift of Pope Pius II. Then comes the fact that in 1462 Antonio was paid for his share in a pair of gorgeous gilt silver and enamel candelabra for the Opera di San Jacopo at Pistoia— a work that Finiguerra and Sali had been engaged in making since 1457—suggests that the apprentice Antonio had become his master's partner. On that occasion, getting paid was not simple, and the stingy Pistoia commissioners raised difficulties that Antonio failed to entirely resolve, even after Piero de' Medici intervened in his favour. Concurrently the pages of the diary of Filippo Rinuccini who, in 1461 and 1462 purchased silver buckles and other women's jewels from Pollaiuolo, give an intimation of a more routine activity that probably insured the prosperity of the workshop in between major commissions. They are all lost or unidentified works, this being the case for the great majority of the ones Antonio continued to produce in the course of his long career. So, regardless of any "hierarchical" implication or anything to do with the nobility of the techniques, we can easily see that Vasari's claim that goldwork did not "give long life to the toils of its creators" is so true that, had Antonio del Pollaiuolo been content merely to work silver and gold, he would practically be unknown today. Furnishings in precious metals have always suffered the risk of being melted down every time demands of an economic nature arose, or even simply when changes in taste prompted the owners to recover the precious material for other purposes. Ghiberti proved he was fully aware of this problem when he told the story about the ghost-like Gusmin of Cologne, a goldsmith at Louis of Anjou's court, who upon seeing his masterpieces melted down for the mint "for the duke's public needs", was so depressed he withdrew to a convent forever. Even Ghiberti in the autobiography included in his *Commentaries* praised as some of the highest achievements of his craft the great pivial buckles and decorated tiaras executed for the popes; and likewise the mount with ivy shoots and dragons designed for a famous antique gem with *Apollo and Marsyas*, all which have irretrievably disappeared. Some thoughts about the vanity of human affairs must have also distressed Antonio when the fabulous tournament trappings—whereby he had given a modish young Florentine, Benedetto Salutati, the illusion of being one of King Arthur's knights or Charlemagne's paladins when appearing in Piazza Santa Croce for the tournament on 7 February 1469, which was won by Lorenzo de' Medici—were taken apart right after the celebration, and reduced to mere silver and precious stones to be turned into money. Instead he was spared seeing the destruction that in 1500, barely two years after his death, his former pupil and colleague Paolo Sogliani wrought on a fabulous silver and enamel Gospels cover that the priests of Santa Maria del Fiore judged too cumbersome, and melted down to draw material for two new candelabra. So in Antonio del Pollaiuolo's case it is not surprising that the proportion of documented works and surviving works is dramatic: over the span of forty years he produced at least six candelabra and five crosses in silver and enamel, two gilt bronze pyxes, four silver basins and, again in silver, a pyx, a thurible, a chalice, a monumental Gospels cover, three reliquaries, and also the low relief with the *Nativity of Saint John* for the baptistery altar, the helmet for Federico da Montefeltro, Salutati's complete tournament trappings (for horse and rider), and then belts and buckles adorned with precious stones, a sheath enriched with enamels and pearls for a knife, a purse with gold finishings for Cardinal Francesco Gonzaga—not to mention various restorations of sacred and profane silverwork. All that is left for us to see today of this dazzling treasure, this sort of Ali Baba's cave, is the panel of the silver altar, the baptistery cross, and a few enamels detached from a second cross that belonged to the convent of San Gaggio. All the rest is gone and probably very little remained already fifty years after Antonio's death; the worst blow dealt to it came during the siege of 1529–30 that was to bring the Medici back to power in Florence, when the Republican government ordered that all gold and silver works, ecclesiastical as well as private, be melted down for coins.

pl. 1

pl. 21

If we think about it, on reading the records of commissions and payments, mostly attentive to the mercantile aspect, the sheer weight of silver, gold, pearls, sapphires and rubies that were used for Antonio's lost goldwork testifies to its glory. That said, rather than for the preciousness of the materials employed, Antonio's work must have stood out on the scene of contemporary gold craftsmanship for the extraordinary scope and quality of the figured parts, with their wealth of cast, carved, or embossed Herculeses, Virtues, angels, and dragons.

In short, the evidence of the documents proves beyond any doubt that the elder Pollaiuolo's craft was first and foremost goldwork, as he was always defined "aurifex" in the records of commissions and payments, account books, and tax returns. Sadly, this means that the essential part of his creative output is lost for us forever.

PAINTINGS BY ANTONIO

At any event, it was actually in 1460, right in the midst of all this flurry about crosses and reliquaries, that Antonio del Pollaiuolo was awarded his most important pictorial assignment of all, at least as regards the quality of the patronage: three large paintings with the *Labours of Hercules* for the Palazzo Medici. We have no information about the circumstances of the commission, but if documents are missing, Pollaiuolo himself comes to our rescue the above-mentioned letter to Orsini of 1494, in which he recalls these paintings, specifying that "it was thirty-four years ago [...] that one of my brothers and I did them", that is, exactly in 1460. In the inventory of the Medici palace drawn up at Lorenzo il Magnifico's death in 1492, the *Labours* figure as hanging on the walls of the "main room". We are told they were canvases about three and a half meters square, precisely representing the hero's battles with the Hydra, the Nemean Lion and Antaeus, themes particularly familiar to Antonio who some time later would offer a "pocket" version of them pl. 16 in the two panels presently in the Uffizi. The Medici pictures, like almost all fifteenth-century paintings on that fragile support, were already lost long ago. To have an idea of them we can only depend on some etchings derived from them, and from their impassioned description by Vasari, who naturally ascribes them to Antonio alone. Without any objective confirmation, it seems a waste of time racking our brains over the role of each of the brothers involved, that is, according to widespread opinion, Antonio and Piero. Yet we should not entirely bar the ingenious solution of Emil Moeller, who seventy years ago identified the assistant mentioned by Antonio not as Piero (then eighteen years old) but as a third brother, the mysterious Silvestro. Born around 1434, Silvestro probably died an early death. We know very little about him, except that he was a goldsmith and lived in Pisa for a short time: however, his name appears at the bottom of a magnificent drawing pl. 27 with a bony, languishing *Saint John the Baptist* in the Uffizi that shows he was a remarkable "figure master".

So, in the absence of the Medici *Hercules*, we shall examine the few paintings which, by their obvious diversity from Piero's ascertained works, should remain ascribed to Antonio del Pollaiuolo, datable between the 1450s and mid-1460s, that is before the role of painting was in fact delegated to his younger brother, at least as regards large formats.

pl. 5

In the *Magdalene Borne to Heaven by Angels* of the Staggia Senese parish church—heavily damaged but certainly one of Antonio's most relevant attempts with the brush—the painting, where it can best be appreciated, is luminous but not bright, and swept by a sharp, terse light, very unlike the taste for pictorial glow and exquisiteness

Fig. 1. Antonio del Pollaiuolo, *Crucifixion with Saints Francis and Jerome*, location unknown.

that the circulation of Netherlandish panels was increasingly spreading, even in Florence; the work is certainly more indebted to Domenico Veneziano than to Rogier van der Weyden. It was precisely Domenico (and to a lesser degree Andrea del Castagno) who provided the most explicit reference for young Antonio's painting, and not merely in the broken, pale calcareous, almost lilac-hued rocks, or in the use of a mainly oil technique that Veneziano appears to have particularly contributed to spreading in Florence. Roberto Longhi's temptation to attribute directly to Pollaiuolo the *Saints Francis and John the Baptist*, originally frescoed in Santa Croce, later detached and now in the basilica museum, is highly eloquent in that regard: in this last masterpiece by Domenico Veneziano, which probably preceded by just a few years the Staggia altarpiece, the emphasised foreshortenings, dry modelling of the limbs, and pathos of the expressions are a direct prelude to Antonio's manner. Among the models for the Staggia altarpiece is the wooden *Magdalene* by Donatello, in the Florentine baptistery at the time, which never fails to be mentioned: it appears to be the direct prototype of the scarified wild hermit borne in glory in the painting. Yet in paying tribute to the mighty genius of the old Florentine Renaissance patriarch, Antonio already showed he was on quite another path. To the magmatic throbbing, almost atmospheric corruption of matter that erodes Donatello's late works, he contrasts the exact opposite, a clear line, often visible, as sharp as an electrical discharge, that individuates the form by carving its outline. Hence the thin angular figures, the daring, almost brutal foreshortenings, the elf-like angels of the *Elevation of Magdalene*. The subject is unusual and can be explained by the intense devotion the commissioner of the painting, Bindo di Agnolo Grazzini, who belonged to one of the outstanding families in Staggia, had for the repentant sinner. All his life Ser Bindo, who worked as a notary in Florence, was a generous patron for his home town, where he had a chapel built in the parish church, but also an entire hospital for providing assistance to women, both dedicated to Magdalene. The altarpiece was designed for one or the other of the two places, and the details of its style suggest it be dated to the late 1450s. Earlier we have a small *Crucifixion*, which today we know only by a reproduction [fig. 1], a clearly devotional work, still rather harsh in its forms but already marked by a graphic acuteness that exacerbates the pathos displayed by the protagonists.

NUDES

Confirmed by the success of the cross for the baptistery, and the *Labours of Hercules* for the Medici, in the early 1460s Antonio had become one of the leading avant-garde figures on the Florentine scene, eclipsing the older masters. Accuracy of outline rather than sophisticated grace likened him to the productions of his peers working in marble, Antonio Rossellino, Desiderio da Settignano, and Mino da Fiesole, and almost straight away he recognised Andrea del Verrocchio as his true rival, and in some regards his *alter ego*.

Antonio's good fortunes must have been significantly supported by the constant affection and lavish attention that the brothers Jacopo and Giovanni Lanfredini always bestowed on him. Powerful men, bankers and diplomats, and close friends of the Medici, the Lanfredini's influence affected Pollaiuolo from the very start, when Jacopo answered for the young goldsmith commissioned for the silver cross. In 1462 Jacopo would also go to the trouble to write to Pistoia to request that the artist be paid for the two candelabra executed for San Jacopo, stressing on the one hand the esteem and consideration Piero de Cosimo de' Medici himself had for Antonio, and on the other insisting on his own friendship ("as for myself I am as fond of him as of a brother"), without hesitating to define Pollaiuolo as "the leading master in this city [...] and this is the opinion shared by all the connoisseurs". It may well be that the Lanfredini were the ones to suggest to Piero de' Medici to use Pollaiuolo for the Hercules canvases, and it was for his protectors that Antonio would take up his brushes again a few years later to decorate the ground-floor room of their suburban Villa at Arcetri on the hills overlooking Florence from the south [fig. 2]. The original wall-painting was discovered under plasterwork toward the end of the nineteenth century, but the opening of a door in the wall had created a large gap in the middle of the painting. Mainly executed in *secco*, today it is severely impaired, but nevertheless we can appreciate the wild, unexpected, disturbing saraband of five nude boys—unmistakably Pollaiuolo's style—so unmistakable that the correct attribution was given by Mary Logan as soon as it was found in 1897, an attribution that has never been challenged since. A short while later the villa passed into the hands of Stefano Bardini, the touchy monarch of Florentine antique trade, who wrought radical alterations on the structures and effectuated a massive restoration on the mural. Yet far more damage was caused by the protracted abandon that ensued and lasted until recently. Composed with arduous foreshortenings, upheld only by the infallible incisiveness of the sign, the five Arcetri dancers are the closest relatives to the Staggia angels, and must have been painted in those same years. These enigmatic dancers, whose meaning has yet to be fathomed, prove the ripening of Antonio's interest for what was to be the guideline of most of his career: the nude figure in movement. Vasari acknowledges that "his knowledge of nudes was more modern than the other masters before him", attributing to him anatomical knowledge learned on dissection tables, but already "Prospectivo Melanese", writing probably while Antonio was still alive, commented on the bronze figures placed on the tomb of Sixtus IV, praising the "anatomy and every nerve and bone as Praxiteles would have done".

In the large number of Pollaiuolesque nudes rendered in the most varied techniques we may be able to identify an evolution: harsher bodies, described in the details of an anatomy under constant tension with a wild, almost ferocious expressivity verging on caricature, developed into a more refined race of imaginary heroes, endowed with impossible physiques, chests so expanded they almost burst, tiny waists, slender nervous biceps, thin supple tapering legs. At the same time expressive means are reduced to essentials and every descriptive procrastination is abandoned to the benefit of an ever thinner line, barring any complementary signs, a pure definition of form obtained through subtraction, that suggests flesh and volumes and hollows merely by a nervous line incising their contours.

Among the most celebrated outcomes of Antonio's experiments on the theme, pl. 6 the *Battle of the Ten Nudes* holds a special position: a signed etching, exceptional in size and executive virtuosity, whose subject is mysterious. Here the burin dwells so on the description of the masses of muscles, the workings of the joints, that the warriors look like models for an anatomy lesson. Despite the bestial ardour inflaming them they do not achieve the lethal nervous elasticity that would transform the Florence pls. 16–20 and the Berlin *Hercules*, the Uffizi *Adam* or the San Lorenzo *Crucifix* into a race of their own, dancers or swimmers grimacing like felines, in turn languid or dismayed, always uncanny. The *Battle*, his one known etching, gave Pollaiuolo extraordinary fame that spread even beyond Tuscany, producing a blossoming of replicas, variants and quotations that soon crossed the Alps. It is assumed that a copy of this etching was the same "cartonum com quibusdam nudis Poleyoli" that passed through Francesco Squarcione's hands, and therefore was in Padua prior to 1468, the year Mantegna's master died. Alternatively we might think of the Pollaiuolesque composition from which an etching was drawn: although the line of the Padua-style artist who materially etched the plate is flintier and more grotesque, it is obviously Antonio's invention in a period not far from that of his signed print [fig. 3]. In any case, even this way, an early date, not far from 1465, seems the most feasible for the *Battle of the Ten Nudes*.

Fig. 2. Antonio del Pollaiuolo, *Dancing Nudes*, detail, Arcetri (Florence), Villa La Gallina.

SILVER, WOOD, CLAY, SILK

Early in 1464 Antonio del Pollaiuolo rented from Jacopo Baroncelli a large and handsome workshop in Via Vacchereccia that was to become the epicentre of his work. During those same months Maso Finiguerra died, which left Antonio the unrivalled leading "master draughtsman" in Florence. Goldwork was still the main sphere of his activity with several commissions of particular prestige, like two luxurious new silver candelabra with figures and enamels to be placed beside the cross on the baptistery altar, and the reliquary-bust of Saint Octavian for the cathedral of

Volterra in 1467. Yet the most outstanding is the visionary ephemeral exploit of the tournament trappings entirely crafted in gilded silver and enamels that Benedetto Salutati donned on the occasion of the famous jousting tournament in 1469, an event that marked Lorenzo de' Medici's public debut. Salutati's commission offers us the best proof that the two brothers' careers had become separate. In fact Antonio systematically received all the payments related to the horse's caparison, the finishings, the helmet, but instead "Piero del Pollaiuolo painter" was paid separately for the standard, and for that alone, which bore the painting of "a young girl and some ladybugs and spheres, wrapped in modest white veils". In the Pollaiuolo's diversified catalogue there are at least two items that in some way relate to the world of tournaments. One is the Louvre wooden shield on which we see modelled in stucco,

pl. 7 gilded and painted, the figure of *Milon of Croton* the unfortunate athlete of antiquity, who, by then an old man who became trapped while he was breaking the trunk of an oak with his bare hands, and was devoured by wild beasts. The piece in question is obviously a parade weapon, the cultured recollection of an antique shield: the violent expressiveness, daring foreshortening of the face, rather stocky proportions, accurate description of the veins and muscles, all remind us of the wild, howling nudes of the etching, advising to also date the shield to before the sixties. It is an object we can well

pl. 3 imagine grasped by the proud youth Pollaiuolo portrayed in the Bargello terracotta bust, the only surviving exemplar, it would appear, of a genre in which Antonio must have been famous, if Ugolino Verino could thus laud: "Spirantes fundit vultus Antonius aere / signaque de molli vivida fingit humo" (Antonio casts his breathing faces in bronze and models lifelike figures in soft clay). We are still in the context of mock warfare, tournaments and jousts: the youth—lush locks, lips, nose, defiant eyes clearly standing out in a full, tender and almost childish face—is wearing a fantastic cuirass, romantically inspired by the classical world, certainly unthinkable for actually going to battle but ideal for appearing handsome in the ladies' eyes. We can still admire the breastplate with the usual furious nudes (wild and somewhat animalesque like in the etching and the shield of the *Milon*), but the true stroke of genius must have been the helmet, too fragmentary today for us to fully appreciate it: not a crest crowned by a dragon but a dragon forming the crest, a huge lizard directly clinging to the terracotta boy's hair.

Subsequently, Antonio was given a new and different opportunity to express more fully his talents as a draughtsman. He was to provide the cartoons for thirty episodes of the Baptist's life (twenty-seven have survived), which were to be embroidered on the liturgical baptistery hangings by a large group of experts from all over Europe: a

pl. 8 pivial, a planet, and two dalmatics. The scope of the undertaking and quality of the work accomplished, in which even the subtlest colour nuances are reproduced, made a great impression even on a viewer like Giorgio Vasari, who was not easily carried

Fig. 3. Fifteenth-century Paduan artist (after Antonio del Pollaiuolo), *Battle of the Ten Nudes*,
London, British Museum, inv. 1854-6-3-1.

away by this kind of luxury item. According to him "the figures were not less well
executed with the needle than Antonio had painted them with the brush". The
embroiderers were already at work in 1466, when evidently Antonio must have
provided at least a first series of drawings. The hangings were not completed until
1487, though this does not mean Pollaiuolo's inventions took twenty years—it was the
master embroiderers who required all that time for their patient transcription task, not
the draughtsman. Most of the scenes seem in fact stylistically homogeneous and
ascribable to a fairly early period of Antonio's career: full of darting fitful hands and
sharp heads, often viewed from below, draperies broken in countless angular folds,
exotic bizarre headgear. Yet in several episodes the figures attain a more solemn
monumentality while the architectures unfold with unusual grandeur and coherence.
These inventions are obviously owed to a second period to which may well refer a
payment for the designs made to Antonio much later, in 1480. The evolution is
especially noticeable in the outdoor scenes. In almost all the episodes the utter
indifference to any landscape naturalism is striking, with their rocky backdrops set
behind the figures, so bristly and fantastic they would have appealed to Lorenzo
Monaco. However on a couple of occasions, in the *Baptism of the Neophytes* and the
Sermon to the Soldiers, the background suddenly opens onto an immense solemn vista
of valleys and plains furrowed by the curves of a river, while a walled city looms on

the horizon. These are especially pictorial ideas Alesso Baldovinetti had been fond of and that Antonio must have particularly appreciated since they had been adopted and developed by his brother Piero who, between the first and second group for the baptistery, had finally made his public debut.

PIERO DEL POLLAIUOLO, FLORENTINE PAINTER

We do not know where Piero learned to draw. The name of Andrea del Castagno that Vasari wrote presents almost insurmountable chronological obstacles since the presumed pupil was fifteen or sixteen years old at the death of his supposed master in 1457. A particularly appealing alternative is that of Alesso Baldovinetti, who in the 1450s began laying inside sharp, highly accurate graphic outlines glazed translucent coats of milky whites, deep reds, greys lit as with lunar ash. At the same time, with more passion than anyone else in Florence, he tried out the optical innovations of Netherlandish painting. A number of expressions from his repertory, settings aglow with slabs of porphyry and serpentine or views of the Valdarno fading away in the background, were passed on to Piero's painting. Yet the crystal eye of Baldovinetti, the most lasting champion of that "painting of light" whose most inspired interpreter was Domenico Veneziano, in young Pollaiuolo was veiled in turbid glazes, a dark palette prone to ruby red, amber browns, peacock blue, while Alesso's deep concern for perspective would end up discarded. Those river backgrounds Baldovinetti had unfolded time and again behind his *Madonnas and Child* or the *Nativity* painted on a wall of the chiostrino dei Voti at the Annunziata (1460–62) would become a true obsession for Piero. However, the geometric clarity whereby the older master suspends that immensity in a shadowless midday hour, with something naive in the flight of the domelike hills, is broken up under Pollaiuolo's oilier, more liquid brush, where the waters of the Arno seem to exhale sultry golden vapours. As for the figures, Piero certainly learned the most fruitful lesson at home growing up next to his brother of ten years older who, when the younger one was just beginning, was already considered with Verrocchio the most important and avant-garde artist in Florence. And it will not be mere fantasy if we imagine the boy drawing over and over under Antonio's watchful gratified eye, an emblematic example of that "continuous practice" among goldsmiths and painters that Vasari lucidly identifies as one of the foundations of the Florentine artistic scene in the late fifteenth century. Piero's first work is still to be reconstructed since he certainly did not begin with as challenging a task as the panel for the Cardinal of Portugal, his oldest datable essay. Among the things that might come before that undertaking we can point out the *Saint Michael assailing the Dragon* of the Museo Bardini in Florence: the canvas, in a wretched state of conservation and largely overpainted, is usually identified with one of the sides of the standard executed for the Compagnia di Sant'Angelo of Arezzo described with admiration by Vasari.

The funerary chapel raised in San Miniato al Monte in memory of the young cardinal Giacomo, prince of Portugal, who died in Florence on 27 August 1459 at the age of twenty-five, famous for his beauty and almost a saint, drew the most eminent of the Florentine masters to work on a commission of the first order, even royal, and tinged with exoticism. The altarpiece, dazzling with Netherlandish-style optical preciousness, pl. 9 is naturally one of the outstanding elements along with the sepulchre caressingly carved by Antonio Rossellino, Luca della Robbia's *optical* majolica ceiling and the mural decorations largely assigned to Alesso Baldovinetti, except for the two figures of angels that Piero had simply glide onto the entablature of the altarpiece in the act of unveiling it by raising a curtain. It is usually believed the altarpiece and two angels pl. 10 were a documented work by Antonio and Piero working as a pair, even providing the irrefutable proof that the two worked together (which then meant Antonio did almost everything, and Piero was content to ruin the little he could lay his hands on: in the specific case Saint Eustace's head). As a matter of fact these so frequently cited documents are nothing but a single payment to the two brothers on 20 October 1466 for "the work they performed for the chapel", without even specifying whether the payment related to the altarpiece, the angels painted on the wall around it, or to both, or whether it might not instead refer to ulterior furnishings that were then lost. It may well be that in this task Antonio was warrant for his younger brother, just twenty, and engaged here in his very first important essay in the city, as again a few years later would occur for the *Virtues* of the Tribunale di Mercanzia.

The San Miniato altarpiece, presently in the Uffizi, is a costumed, courtly painting. The three actors on the stage, Saints Vincent, James and Eustace, subtly differentiated in age and personality, are bending their sweet melancholy heads, shifting highly sensitive inspired hands in the diffused glow of rubies and pearls studding truly princely garments, in the midst of countless chic inventions like Saint James' luxury pilgrim's hat, or the mock-poor sandals in woven rope, or whimsical refinements like Eustace's emblem (the stag head with the crucifix between the antlers) turned into a design brooch, a hermetic emblem of membership in an exclusive club. This is an entirely different humankind compared to the angular, anxious, expressive little figures Antonio displayed in the baptistery embroideries in those same years. The "Portuguese" altarpiece turned Piero del Pollaiuolo into one of the most prominent painters in Florence, and it was indeed to him the powerful Tribunale di Mercanzia (Guild of Merchants) turned, in the summer of 1469, to have an allegorical figure painted representing *Charity* to be placed in the council room of their premises on Piazza della Signoria. At the end of the year, in front of the completed panel, the counsellors decided to enhance it with six more figures forming a complete cycle of the theological and cardinal *Virtues*. For the first time the Pollaiuolo were faced with their most fearsome rival, Andrea del Verrocchio, whose formation was in many aspects comparable to Antonio's and who had become the Medici's official artist, ousting the poulterer's two sons. Verrocchio, who was in a way playing home field since he recently had been engaged by the same Tribunale di Mercanzia to execute the bronze group of the *Incredulity of Saint Thomas* for the Orsanmichele church, actually presented the drawing for a *Faith*, offering to replace Pollaiuolo for the commission: this time the danger was foiled and the work remained in Piero's hands.

pls. 12–14 However, his haughty ladies, laden with jewels and wearily seated on coloured marbles thrones, never found great favour with the critics. Undoubtedly the countless layers of restorations and overpainting on these images weighed heavily on this judgement, as the recent cleaning of the *Charity* revealed, rendering to the figure a fair share of those pictorial qualities that convinced the sponsors to trust Piero, the glowing deep red of the velvet almost like Gothic stained glass, the textural virtuosity of the brocaded mantle painted as with a needle more than a brush. In the end however, perhaps owing to the slowness with which Piero was proceeding in the task, the young go-getter Sandro Botticelli succeeded in intervening, securing for himself the figure of *Fortitude*. The glory of stuffs and jewels profuse in the *Virtues* also

pl. 11 enriches the Turin canvas with *The Archangel Raphael and Tobias* originally at Orsanmichele in Florence. If Saint Raphael's bored snobbish face is rather bothersome, the endless expanse of golden fields furrowed by the shining river is highly effective, and the hyperrealism of the divine wayfarer's wings superlative: one in full sunlight, soft with ruffled plumage, the other described in every single feather, clearly tactile and magical. Qualities Lorenzo de' Medici himself so appreciated he engaged Piero to portray Galeazzo Maria Sforza, duke of Milan, when the illustrious ally visited Florence in 1471: a painting the Magnifico always kept in his room and that Pollaiuolo, as was practised at Bruges, had composed in three-quarter profile instead of in full profile.

IN THE AGE OF LORENZO IL MAGNIFICO

pl. 23 The *Martyrdom of Saint Sebastian* is the largest, most complex panel of those produced by Piero del Pollaiuolo's workshop. It was made for the altar of the oratory named after that saint which the Pucci family owned in the church of the Annunziata in Florence. Vasari gives its date as 1475—probably based on an inscription visible at the time on the frame or the altar—and presents it as Antonio's masterpiece, but the ensemble of the older testimonies insure us it is also in this case a work by Piero, as

pl. 24 confirmed by the similarity of its style with the signed San Gimignano altarpiece. At that time Antonio had already left large-scale paintings, altarpieces or mural paintings to his brother's skill and his workshop on Piazza degli Agli, saving his own hand for small intimate paintings for rooms in the palaces of the Medici, the Lanfredini and their friends. Actually there are several small Pollaiuolesque panels in which the skilled rendering of pearls and velvets, the oily moist texture, the languid sentimental tone typical of the younger brother's painting yield to a supreme linear definition where the drawing clearly stands out under the colour and articulates the form with a quick supple sign. For instance I think we should maintain as Antonio's the famous female pl. 15 profile of Museo Poldi Pezzoli. The sharp heartless drawing that does not dwell on details but freezes for all time the fussy little nose and pouting lip, accurately weaves the ribbons and strings of pearls in the gossamer-lit hair, is the same as the one that etched the struggle of *Hercules and the Hydra* and *Hercules and Antaeus* in the Uffizi pl. 16 panels. In the two small paintings Antonio, in miniature and in later days, returns to study the old theme of the Medici pictures he would always care for and spell out in the most varied techniques, as we see in the bronze version of *Hercules and Antaeus* in pl. 17 the Museo del Bargello. The group is set on a small triangular base that induces the viewer to constantly change viewpoints, sliding along the sides and swerving around the corners while projections of the lethal embrace are constantly renewed. Thus the increasingly subtle, intense study of the straining human body shifts indifferently from one medium to the next, from small painting to little bronze, from drawing to sculpture, from the two admirable sheets with the Uffizi *Adam* and *Eve* to the Berlin pls. 18, 19 *Hercules resting*, a sample of that Pollaiuolesque race of giant athletes Antonio's uninhibited imagination transposed from mythology to sacred history. Thus the *Crucifix* carved in cork-oak in the basilica of San Lorenzo in Florence looks no less pl. 20 heroic than Hercules: a figure of great expressive intensity that overcomes the conventions of such a binding traditional iconography, both in the face's grimace of pain and the diver's body about to fly off the cross.

At the height of his expressive skill, mastering every technique, in the 1470s Antonio develops to the utmost the graphic tension that defines the figure, articulates it in space, exasperates its power, makes the features pungent and extremely sharp with a sign that instantly turns into action, even by a mere angular twist of a heel or a sudden spring of the loins. On the other hand Piero, entirely devoted to painting, remains true to the Netherlandish lesson, to the sheen of pearls and satins, smooth caressing oils that polish limbs and enervate countenances. Of course being the younger brother of the most renowned draughtsman in Florence, it is not surprising he was his foremost devotee as well, all the more so in a "heroic" painting like *Saint Sebastian* pl. 23 where he had the opportunity to show off his own anatomical skill. Yet the frail martyr and his robust tormenters alike are completely lacking in Antonio's synthesis of energy. All we appreciate about their bodies veiled in golden light is surface accidents, consistency of flesh, surfacing of bones, translucent tracery of veins under the skin. However, Piero's greatest gifts are expressed in the background, the valley furrowed by the waters (this time to be interpreted as the Tiber) with brown-spotted fields and the distant horizon drenched in sunlight. We have the same sentimental tone and same palette in one of the paintings that has always been tenaciously attributed to Antonio but definitely ought to be given back to his brother: the pl. 22 London panel with *Apollo and Daphne* in which the metamorphosis takes place before the eyes of the little god in his embroidered silk vest over a hazy view of damp riverbanks and periwinkle-blue hills.

Antonio and Piero were by then famous and well-established in the circles of the Medici and their intimates. It was with inconceivable satisfaction that more and more often they saw their names Latinised and placed next to those of Apelles and Praxiteles in the poems and letters of intellectuals connected with Lorenzo: Ugolino Verino, Antonio Ivani and above all Marsilio Ficino, who appears to have been a particularly close friend of the two brothers. Their fame (especially Antonio's) went beyond the boundaries of the Tuscan State, and the helmet offered to Federico da Montefeltro after the siege of Volterra so pleased the duke of Urbino that he claimed in a letter sent to Florence to the Magnifico: "I couldn't say how much I love this Antonio and how willingly I would do anything to please him" (23 May 1473). Fame also brought an increase in their earnings, and their tax returns to the cadastre for the year 1480 provide a photograph of the definitely prosperous material conditions of the two brothers. Antonio, 49 years old, is married to a Marietta twenty years younger and is childless. He resides on his own property with his brothers Piero and Giovanni, owns plenty of houses and land especially in the county of Pistoia where for some time he had concentrated his investments, and works in the Via Vacchereccia goldsmith workshop with someone always at his side (at the time the young partner Paolo Sogliani). Instead Piero is a bachelor (he will never marry but will have an illegitimate daughter) committed to supporting their mother, now aged, and he, too, has some small property in the Pistoia area; he rents the workshop in Piazza degli Agli "that I use when I have to paint". Connections with Pistoia where the two are obviously at home are beneficial for new work opportunities as well, even though they missed the tastiest morsel when in 1477 the Pistoiese wished to raise a monument in the cathedral to the memory of their fellow citizen cardinal Niccolò Forteguerri, born and buried in Rome and prodigal of benefits for his home town. At first, among the five models presented, Verrocchio's was chosen, but his economic requests deeply embarrassed the local administrators. The ones responsible for the commission, "understanding Piero del Pollaiuolo to be here", turned to him for an alternative project and once they obtained it deemed it "more beautiful and worthier of art", winning the praise of the deceased's brother and the entire

Forteguerri family (mind you this enthusiasm is a bit doubtful since it is clear that at Pistoia they cared more for saving money than for the "beauty" and "dignity" of the work). But since Verrocchio protested and the Florentine magistrates of the city sided with him they had the notion of writing to ask Lorenzo de' Medici's opinion, joining the two projects, "because of such things and of all others you have the fullest understanding". The hope to convince Lorenzo in favour of Piero over Andrea just shows how little Pistoia knew about the Medici's taste, since they had been Verrocchio's greatest protectors for ages. The episode, which as we can see had important political implications and involved well-known persons, raises some doubts about young Pollaiuolo's intentions. Neither the documents nor his works enable us to believe he was ever a sculptor: did he plan to just make the model leaving the execution up to others? Or instead to satisfy the Pistoiese's wish to save, had he proposed a painted cenotaph?

The confrontation between the two greatest goldsmiths, bronze sculptors, draughtsmen of Lorenzo's Florence, Antonio del Pollaiuolo and Andrea Verrocchio, that almost occurred at least twice and always through Piero (in 1470 for the Mercanzia *Virtues*, in 1477 for the Forteguerri affair), took place at last in 1478 when they shared the work to complete the silver altar of the Florentine baptistery. They were to execute the four panels with episodes from the life of the Baptist that would occupy the flanks of the work, two on each side. The task was divided between four workshops, and Antonio and Andrea were respectively assigned the *Nativity* and the *Beheading*, consigned, late, in 1480. All in all, the *Nativity of the Baptist* is not one of Antonio del Pollaiuolo's most successful pieces. The composition duplicates the idea already used for the embroidery of the same subject, but the grandly architectural setting is then betrayed by an execution that is not quite mastered. We might suspect Antonio left room for his new workshop companion, young Paolo Sogliani, with whom he had entered in partnership on 19 November 1477, obviously in view of the important commission. The fact that the final payment was expressly made to "Antonio del Pollaiuolo and companion, goldsmiths" seems to confirm the assumption. Undoubtedly Verrocchio comes out the winner of the competition both in the dramatic effectiveness of his *Martyrdom* and display of faultlessly chiselled antique-style helmets and cuirasses. A collaborator's less inspired hand can also be clearly seen in the enamels that in the same years Antonio had executed for a silver cross of the convent of San Gaggio and which, exceptionally, have come down to us, although detached a long time ago and remounted in a modest sixteenth-century brass crucifix (Florence, Museo del Bargello). Of the six surviving figures only four are autograph, and they are the ones where the quality soars, as in the *God the Father* pl. 21 or *Saint John Grieving*, contracted in a spasm of grief that convulses his features and petrifies his hands pressed on the cascading folds of the mantle.

For Piero instead these seem to be rather hard times. After the success of *Saint*
Sebastian he missed a couple of public opportunities. On 24 December 1477 he was
commissioned for the altarpiece for the San Bernardo chapel in the Palazzo della
Signoria; but just a few days later, without our being able today to know the reason,
the engagement was revoked and transferred first to Leonardo and then (in 1483) to
Ghirlandaio (the painting was never executed anyway). Four years later, in October
1482, Piero was involved in another project for the Palazzo Vecchio, frescoing the Sala
dei Signori (today called "Sala dei Gigli", i.e., Hall of the Lilies), where he was to do
the south wall while Ghirlandaio, Botticelli and the pair formed by Perugino and
Biagio d'Antonio, all fresh from their Roman experience on the scaffolds of the
Sistine Chapel, were to work on the three other walls. But once again things did not
go according to plan and the occasion fell through without our understanding why:
Ghirlandaio would be the only one to execute the commission. Thereupon, in 1483,
Piero signed and dated the altarpiece of the high altar of Sant'Agostino at San
Gimignano. This large resplendent *Coronation of the Virgin* is without a shadow of a
doubt the most neglected work of the entire corpus ascribed to the two Pollaiuolo
brothers, condemned by Vasari's silence to be perpetually left out of the discussion or,
if mentioned, unfailingly deprecated and even derided, precisely because of Piero's
signature that stands out so markedly. An unprejudiced comparison between the
Augustinian panel and far more praised paintings, like that of the Cardinal of Portugal
or the London *Saint Sebastian* proves instead such an exact match in style and
technique as to imply they are by the same hand. The Berlin Pinakothek *Annunciation*
must also belong to the same period as the San Gimignano panel: a painting certainly
conceived for a very prestigious destination judging by the extreme executive
refinement and ostentation of luxury in the setting, but we know nothing about its
provenance or the hands it passed through. Conversely the large canvas with *Saint*
Antoninus Worshipping the Crucifix created for the sepulchre of the Florentine
Dominican saint in the church of San Marco and now in the adjacent museum,
presents a more complex attribution problem. In 1510 Albertini mentioned it as a
work by Piero, forty years later Vasari ascribed it to Antonio. After the late sixteenth
century when the chapel was turned into the grandiose room we can still admire
today, every trace of the fifteenth-century canvas disappeared. When in 1907 Odoardo
Giglioli finally found it, hidden in the convent, he proposed to attribute it to Alesso
Baldovinetti, an idea that was widely popular until more recently Luciano Bellosi and
Everett Fahy suggested it might be an early work by Francesco Botticini. And in fact
today the debate still hesitates between Baldovinetti and Botticini. Instead I wonder,
for the very damaged painting, whether we should not seriously reconsider Albertini's
reference to Piero del Pollaiuolo. If we strain to see beyond its wretched state of
conservation, the canvas appears to present a quality far superior to Botticini's, who at
the most seems to have been inspired by this image on several occasions and especially

pl. 23
pl. 24
pl. 9
pl. 23
pl. 25
pl. 26

in a small panel at the Alte Pinakothek of Munich that punctually derives from it. Nor should we ignore the testimony of the Dominican Serafino Razzi. Compiling a chronicle of the convent in 1586 he confirmed the paternity of "Pollaiuolo Florentine painter", even specifying the year of its execution, 1483, and the name of the patron, the prior Francesco Salviati.

But Piero is about to leave the scene: the last evidence concerning him goes back to 18 November 1485, when his brother had already moved to Rome to design the monument for Pope Sixtus IV. At that date he was paid for a panel, not identified, for the Corpus Domini chapel in the Duomo of Pistoia, funds that Piero immediately put to use purchasing a new property in the Pistoiese *contado* where the family real estate ambitions were already directed. We cannot specify the exact date of his death, certainly before November 1496 when Antonio in dictating his will mentioned him as dead some time before.

IN ROME

It sounds as if Antonio had not yet ever visited Rome, given that the newly appointed Florentine ambassador to the Holy See, Giovanni Lanfredini, wrote him an affectionate letter on 28 May 1484, asking him to join him in the capital, describing in impassioned terms the ruined splendour of the antiquities. Antonio soon travelled down to Rome, and drawing him there may not have just been "the many ruins and remains that evidence fabulous greatness" but above all the news of the imminent death of the pope, Sixtus IV Della Rovere, who had been lying ill in bed for months now and for whose tomb something unusual and grand was being planned by his extremely ambitious nephew, the cardinal Giuliano. The commission from Pollaiuolo of a work of such utter prestige must have been wagered in the course of a clever diplomatic game, which certainly involved Giovanni Lanfredini, and probably even the participation of Lorenzo de' Medici, whose relationship with the Ligurian pope after the serious crisis following the Pazzi conspiracy in 1478 had been mended, also by means of a number of artistic diplomatic missions, beginning with the team of painters sent by the Magnifico to paint the walls of the large papal chapel that Sixtus had rebuilt in the Vatican Palaces. The pope finally died on 12 August 1484 and the Florentine artist must have set to work right away on what everyone knew would be the most memorable undertaking of a memorable career.

Extremely new in conception, entirely free-standing, and destined to occupy the centre of the princely chapel that Sixtus had installed in Saint Peter's during his lifetime, the Della Rovere tomb immediately enjoyed a special fame and was pl. 28

celebrated in verse and prose far more than would be the case of the later monument to Innocent VIII (perhaps also because in praising the monument its patron, Cardinal Giuliano, raised to Pope Julius II in 1503, was praised at the same time). A success that never waned until the classicist tendencies of Leopoldo Cicognara, who preferred Innocent VIII's more orthodox monument, took over. Later the bigoted nineteenth century was scandalized by the lack of holy figures in the tomb's rich iconography, but pls. 29 even more by the way Antonio imagined the allegories of the Virtues, the Arts, and the Sciences as half-dressed girls that accompany the effigy, with its amazingly realistic countenance, of the dead Franciscan pope. We should not forget however that, in its original position, the unusual bronze work dialogued with the *Virgin in Glory Worshipped by the Pontiff* frescoed by Pietro Perugino in the apse of the mortuary chapel, sacrificed in 1610 to the advance of the new Saint Peter's. Such a daring conception perfectly suited Giuliano's personality, almost as though he had already been imagining the projects he would conceive for his own person, once elected pope, doubling their grandeur and assigning them to Michelangelo.

Antonio was a practical man with good business sense, and even in his years in Rome he always kept up his connections with his native city, appearing in Tuscany every time business or the administration of his significant possessions required, with a facility to set off on a journey that quite amazes us today. There were rents to collect, harvests to estimate, and above all houses and land to buy, because his investments, still concentrated essentially in the Pistoia area, went on uninterruptedly. But in Florence there was especially the goldsmith workshop in Via Vacchereccia to manage: the firm had never shut down, as the various commissions of crosses and chalices prove, although in those years it was mostly Paolo Sogliani who ran it.

In Rome the social level of Antonio's commissions had risen considerably. The families of the good society of Florence, the Lanfredini, the Salutati, were replaced by the most prominent cardinals of the Curia, such as Giuliano Della Rovere, Lorenzo Cybo and Virginio Orsini, whom Antonio proposed to portray in a bronze bust, or perhaps even in an equestrian portrait. Meanwhile, from Milan, Ludovico il Moro consulted him, probably through his cardinal brother Ascanio Sforza, for the design for an equestrian monument in memory of his father, whom Antonio envisioned daringly rearing over the fallen enemy in two study drawings that have reached us (presently in Munich and New York). When the artist was back in Florence, the Magnifico met him personally, entrusted him with secret diplomatic missions, tended to his interests and, once back in Rome, kept up a correspondence with him. An estimate of the relationship between the two Pollaiuolo and the Medici family can be drawn up on the grounds of the inventory of the family palace after Lorenzo's death on 8 April 1492. We can see the old canvases with the three *Labours of Hercules*, the

Fig. 4. Anonymous early-seventeenth-century artist, *The Funerary Monument to Innocent VIII in its original disposition*, Berlin, Kupferstichkabinett, inv. 620.

bronze *Hercules and Antaeus*, the portrait pl. 17 of Galeazzo Maria Sforza. Antonio's relationship with the new head of the Medici family never became that close: Piero di Lorenzo probably lost sight of this ageing artist, who had been living in Rome most of the time for the past ten years, and Pollaiuolo had to ask his Roman protectors, Giuliano Della Rovere (in 1493), and Gentil Virginio Orsini (in 1494), to write a letter recommending him to the new, though short-lived, master of Florence.

In the last stage of his career, Antonio extended his already very wide range of interests and skills to include architecture, with designs and advice most of which eludes us today. In May 1495 he presented to the Operai di Santo Spirito in Florence a model for the dome of their sacristy (but the work collapsed on 5 September), and between the summer and the autumn of the same year, again in Florence, he had a series of meetings with the Pistoiese architect Ventura Vitoni, and with Antonio da Sangallo, over the construction of the church of Santa Maria dell'Umiltà in Pistoia. But in Rome the final task now awaited him, Innocent VIII's Funerary Monument, whose pl. 31 commission was a natural sequel to the triumph of Sixtus's tomb. The Cybo family did not share the utopian grandeur of Giuliano Della Rovere's imagination, and preferred the more traditional design of the wall monument, completing however the allegories of the Virtues and the image of the recumbent pope with a second effigy of Innocent, alive and enthroned, after models practised in the fourteenth century for royal or imperial tombs: an innovation that would affect the design of successive pontifical funerary monuments. In the original plan, Innocent's tomb was to be in close connection with the ciborium that contained the tip of the spear with which the centurion was said to have pierced Jesus' breast on the day of the Crucifixion. It was one of the Vatican's most precious relics, and had reached Rome in 1492 as an unexpected diplomatic gift from the Turkish sultan, Bajazet II; the statue of the pope pl. 32 actually submits it for the worship of the faithful. We cannot claim that the two monuments appear today in the most favourable way: the Della Rovere pope's is sunk in the rather gloomy shadow of the modern Museo del Tesoro in the Vatican, while the Cybo pope's, altered in the seventeenth century [fig. 4], is attached to a pillar of the south nave of Saint Peter's—a rare vestige of the antique Constantinian basilica built alongside the new one—in the midst of stretches of marbles and huge stuccoes that hardly suit its gilded bronze refinement. And yet in the perfect balance between grandiose conception and accurate finishing of detail, the two monuments are there to demonstrate Antonio's skill in plying the subtleties of his formation as a goldsmith to a new celebrative dimension, a grandiloquent, intensely ideological language. Then in the individual figures, the dry, vital humanity that had always lived in his imagination, unfolds with incomparable variety and energy, for once entirely female.

pl. 29

Antonio del Pollaiuolo wrote his will in Rome on 4 November 1496. A man of his time, it distressed him not to have had any male children, but he made careful provisions so that his heirs—his second wife and two daughters, Marietta and Maddalena—would not be done out of their inheritance by his brother Giovanni's sons, the only male descendants of the family. He lived another year and three months, finally dying in the papal city on 4 February 1498. Ten days later from Florence, now under Republican government, instructions arrived for the ambassador Domenico Bonsi to back the requests of Lucrezia, widow of the "famous sculptor [...] our citizen and man unique in his art", to her husband's creditors. As expressed in his last wishes Pollaiuolo's remains were buried in the basilica of San Pietro in Vincoli in Rome, directly to the left on entering. With an unusual ostentation for a fifteenth-century artist, the tomb is illustrated by a wall monument on which the countenances of Antonio and Piero stand out carved in marble, while the epitaph celebrates in Latin the glory of the "fictor insignis" everlastingly associated with the pontifical bronzes. The modest sculptor who executed the work must have known Antonio well, or perhaps had seen the man's death mask, so incisive is the rendering of this elderly head. With its prominent nose and small sharp eyes it matches the portrait Filippino Lippi had left of Antonio in the *Stories of Saint Peter* in the Brancacci chapel a short while before Pollaiuolo left for Rome, almost as if wishing the keep his memory alive among his colleagues in the *sancta sanctorum* of the Florentine Renaissance. Conversely, Piero's bust is that of a man in his youth, with idealized features and an engrossed expression, a melancholy act of affection toward his younger, less gifted brother, prematurely passed away, whom Antonio wanted to keep by his side in eternity.

LIST OF PLATES

pl. 1. Antonio del Pollaiuolo and Betto di Francesco Betti, *Silver Cross* of the baptistery, 1457–59, silver and enamels, h. 250 cm, Florence, Museo dell'Opera di Santa Maria del Fiore.
Commissioned in 1457 by the Arte di Calimala (the wool and textile guild), the cross was Antonio's first major assignment: he did not yet have his own *bottega* and was "working" in that of Miliano Dei; at the time of settlement Pollaiuolo received 2,006 florins for the lower part, Betto 1,030 for the upper part. Antonio himself was to execute in 1465–70 two candelabra, also in silver and enamels, to flank the cross on the altar of the baptistery (lost).

pl. 2. Antonio del Pollaiuolo, *Harpy*, detail of the *Silver Cross* of the baptistery, 1457–59, silver, Florence, Museo dell'Opera di Santa Maria del Fiore...
Information regarding a restoration on the cross in the early eighteenth century performed by Bernardo Holzman led to longstanding reservations regarding the two figures of harpies placed on the base, believed to have been added on that occasion. Actually they are stupendous creations by Antonio, impressive for the intense features, and the proud, almost glowering heads, with their thick curly locks.

pl. 3. Antonio del Pollaiuolo, *Bust of a Youth Wearing a Ceremonial Suit of Armour*, ca. 1460–70, terracotta, h. 50 cm, Florence, Museo Nazionale del Bargello, inv. 166 M.
Lacking both arms, the piece entered the Bargello in 1864; previously in the hospital of Santa Maria Nuova, its original destination and the identity of the sitter are still unknown. There is no reason to believe it is a piece of a complete figure, nor even less that it is a fake, as has been claimed. The bust was immensely popular in the late nineteenth century, when many replicas of it were cast.

pl. 4. Antonio del Pollaiuolo, *The Baptism of Christ*, detail of the *Silver Cross* of the baptistery, 1457–59, embossed silver, Florence, Museo dell'Opera di Santa Maria del Fiore.
The plaque, that is on the front side of the cross at the centre of the neck of the foot, lost its coloured enamel facing (a small portion remains in the lower left corner). The *Baptism*, along with the figure beneath it of *Moses Enthroned*, is the very finest image of all the enamelwork for which payment was made to Antonio, who already on this occasion obviously had the assistance of collaborators.

pl. 5. Antonio del Pollaiuolo, *Magdalene Borne to Heaven by Angels*, ca. 1460, tempera and oil on wooden panel, 209.5 x 166.2 cm, Staggia Senese, Museo del Pollaiuolo.
It came to the museum from the parish church of Santa Maria. The patron was Bindo Grazzini, a notary born at Staggia but working in Florence, with a special devotion for Magdalene, for whom he named a chapel in the parish church but also the small hospital he had built in his home town. Forgotten for a long time, the altarpiece was pointed out in 1899 by Guido Carocci and then published with due emphasis by Berenson in 1905.

pl. 6. Antonio del Pollaiuolo, *Battle of the Ten Nudes*, ca. 1460–65, etching, 42.4 x 60.9 cm, Cleveland, The Cleveland Museum of Art, inv. 1967. 127.
Signed "OPUS / ANTONII POLLA / IOLI FLORENT / TINI" in the *tabula ansata* hanging on a tree on the left. Almost 50 copies have been conserved, but the only print of the first state is the one in the Cleveland Museum of Art. The subject has still not been elucidated despite the efforts of many, including Panofsky. The two warriors who are struggling in the centre over a chain are the same figure in front and rear view, according to a device both Antonio and Piero favoured.

pl. 7. Antonio del Pollaiuolo, *Milon of Croton*, ca. 1465, painted and gilded stucco on wood, Paris, Musée du Louvre, inv. OA 7381.
Framed by the inscription: "SAPIENTIS EST POST VICTORIA[M] QUIESCERE. NIHIL N[AM] TAM FIRMU[M] CUI NO[N] SIT PERICULU[M] AB INVALIDO" (the second part is drawn from the *Storia di Alessandro Magno* by Curzio Rufo, VII, 8). The coat of arms at lower right has never been plausibly identified. The shield was in the Capel Cure collection of Badger Hall, auctioned in London in 1905; it entered the Louvre in 1921 with the donation of Godefroy Brauer.

pl. 8. After Antonio del Pollaiuolo, *The Naming of Saint John the Baptist*, ca. 1466–69, silk and gold thread embroidery, 22 x 30 cm, Florence, Museo dell'Opera di Santa Maria del Fiore.
It belongs to the series of 27 embroideries on the white brocade (pivial, planet, and two dalmatics) used for the solemn celebrations of Saint John, in the Florentine baptistery. The team of embroiderers was composed of Netherlanders and Venetians, Spaniards and Veronese, French and Florentines. Detached from the consumed original liturgical robes during the eighteenth century, the *Stories of Saint John the Baptist* entered the museum at the time of its creation, in 1891.

pl. 9. Piero del Pollaiuolo, *Saints Vincent, James, and Eustace* (altarpiece of the Cardinal of Portugal), ca. 1466–67, oil on wood, 172 x 179 cm, Florence, Galleria degli Uffizi, inv. 1617.
In the Uffizi collections since 1800, the painting comes from the funerary chapel of James of Portugal, Cardinal of Sant'Eustachio, in San Miniato al Monte. The name of the deceased and his title explain the choice of two of the saints, whereas the third, Vincent of Saragossa, is especially worshipped in Lisbon. The frame *all'antica* is the original, carved by Giuliano da Maiano. An enamelled plaque inlaid at the centre of the trabeation and bearing the cardinal's coat of arms is clearly a work by Antonio.

pl. 10. Piero del Pollaiuolo, *Angel Opening a Curtain*, ca. 1466–67, oil on masonry, Florence, San Miniato al Monte, chapel of the Cardinal of Portugal.
This angel and a second one, obtained by reversing the same cartoon, are Piero's sole contribution to the decoration of the walls of the chapel, the rest being by Alesso Baldovinetti. Executed in oil on the wall, a technique that allows greater pictorial nuances but is far less enduring than fresco, the paintings are badly damaged. The angels are shown gliding in the votive chapel, their feet touching the altarpiece and drawing aside a heavy red curtain

pl. 11. Piero del Pollaiuolo, *The Archangel Raphael and Tobias*, ca. 1465–70, oil on wood, 188 x 119 cm, Turin, Galleria Sabauda, inv. 117.
Not cited in the oldest sources, it is mentioned by Vasari on a pillar of the church of Orsanmichele, but he inaccurately quoted the support as being canvas. Gaetano Milanesi found it in the Florentine Palazzo dei Tolomei, in Via Ginori; here Baron Hector de Garriod purchased it for the Galleria Sabauda of Turin, where it arrived in 1865.

pl. 12. Piero del Pollaiuolo, *Temperance*, 1470, oil on wood, 167 x 88 cm, Florence, Galleria degli Uffizi, inv. 497.
It belongs to the series of the *Virtues* for the Sala del Consiglio of the Tribunale di Mercanzia (Guild of Merchants), in Piazza della Signoria: *Temperance*, mixing cold and hot water, was paid to Piero on 2 August 1470. The seven panels (six by Pollaiuolo, plus *Fortitude* by Sandro Botticelli) entered the Uffizi in 1717.

pl. 13. Piero del Pollaiuolo, *Prudence*, 1470 or 1471, oil on wood, 167 x 88 cm, Florence, Galleria degli Uffizi, inv. 496.
It wields the traditional attributes of this Virtue: the snake, and the mirror to see behind her back. In the nineteenth century this was the only one of the Mercanzia allegories to be shown in the Uffizi because it was the only one in a satisfactory state of conservation. The piece has been improved by a very recent restoration (2004).

pl. 14. Piero del Pollaiuolo, *Head of Faith*, 1470, black and red pencil on paper, 21.1 x 18.2 cm, Florence, Galleria degli Uffizi, Gabinetto Disegni e Stampe, inv. 14506 F.
Preparatory for one of the figures of the *Virtues* of the Tribunale di Mercanzia, the drawing was pricked along the outer contours to transfer the tracing on the panel by the technique of *spolvero* (pouncing). Today the skilful, delicate use of the coloured pencils renders a better notion of Piero's qualities than the atching painting, one of the most damaged and retouched of the cycle.

pl. 15. Antonio del Pollaiuolo (?), *Young Girl in Profile*, ca. 1470–75, tempera and oil (?) on wood, 45.5 x 32.7 cm, Milan, Museo Poldi Pezzoli, inv. 442/157.
It used to bear on the reverse the inscription "Uxor Johannis de Bardi", removed during a nineteenth-century restoration because deemed apocryphal. It is the loveliest and most famous of a series of women's portraits (Berlin, Staatliche Museen; New York, Metropolitan Museum; Florence, Uffizi; Boston, Isabella Stewart Gardner Museum) still highly disputed between Antonio and Piero, and certainly not all by the same hand.

pl. 16. Antonio del Pollaiuolo, *Hercules and the Hydra*, ca. 1470–80, oil on wood, 17.5 x 12 cm, Florence, Galleria degli Uffizi, inv. 8268.
It forms a pair with the small panel representing *Hercules and Antaeus*; they appear together in a 1609 inventory of the collection of Benedetto Gondi in Florence, joined in a diptych "ad uso di libro che si serra" (for use as in a book that closes). They came to the Uffizi in 1798 from the Palazzo Pitti, were stolen in 1943, and recovered in Los Angeles in 1962. They duplicate, some ten years later, the theme of the canvases executed in 1460 for the Palazzo Medici.

pl. 17. Antonio del Pollaiuolo,
Hercules and Antaeus,
ca. 1470–75, bronze, h. 46 cm,
Florence, Museo Nazionale
del Bargello, inv. 280 B.
The piece is usually identified with
a bronze recorded in the Palazzo
Medici 1492 inventory, although
it has been observed that the
measurements do not match,
and the appraisal declared
(2 florins) seems oddly low.
The composition, already utilised
by Antonio in the lost canvases
for Piero de' Medici, and in a
small panel now in the Uffizi,
would later inspire etchings
(Cristofano Robetta), majolicas,
marquetries, and other paintings
(Matteo di Giovanni, New Haven,
Jarves Collection).

pl. 18. Antonio del Pollaiuolo,
Adam, ca. 1470–80, black pencil,
pen and watercolour on paper,
28.3 x 17.9 cm, Florence,
Galleria degli Uffizi, Gabinetto
Disegni e Stampe, inv. 95F.
The drawing forms a pair with
the *Eve with the infants Cain and
Abel*, also in the Uffizi, to which
it was perhaps originally joined.
The destination and purpose of
these drawings are not known,
but it may well be they were
considered finished works.
Copies and quotations attest
their popularity in the past:
Fiorella Sricchia pointed out
the very accurate ones of the
lovely *Flagellation* of the Museo
Capitolare in Atri, a work
by the Maestro di Bolea.

pl. 19. Antonio del Pollaiuolo,
Hercules Resting,
ca. 1475–80, bronze,
h. 40.5 cm, Berlin, Staatliche
Museen, inv. 3043.
The small bronze was purchased
by Wilhelm Bode in London in
1907, its provenance being the
collection of Alfred Beit. Hercules
has his feet on the hide of the
Nemean lion and is holding the
apples of the Hesperides in his left
hand. The *tabula ansata* hanging
on a nail on the base, oddly
enough, does not feature
an inscription.

pl. 20. Antonio del Pollaiuolo,
Crucifix, ca. 1470–80,
cork-oak, 160 x 160 cm,
Florence, San Lorenzo.
Recorded by Vasari as a work
by the mythical Simone, brother
of Donatello, in San Basilio degli
Armeni, after the suppression
of that church it was removed
to San Lorenzo. It has been given
all manner of attributions (Baccio
da Montelupo, Simone Ferrucci,
even Donatello) before Margrit
Lisner reassigned it to Antonio.
The crucifix is carved out of cork
to make it easier to carry
during processions.

pl. 21. Antonio del Pollaiuolo,
God the Father and *Saint John
Grieving*, 1477–80,
enamel on silver,
8.1 x 8.1 cm each, Florence,
Museo Nazionale del Bargello,
inv. OR 15.
The two pieces originally belonged
to the silver cross in the monastery
of San Gaggio, by the gates
of Florence, for which there are
payments to Antonio between
1477 and 1479. In the first half
of the sixteenth century the
plaques were remounted, with
four other remaining pieces,
on a modest gilded copper cross,
that entered the Bargello museum
in 1867. Only a few traces of
the original translucent enamel
facing are left.

pl. 22. Piero del Pollaiuolo,
Apollo and Daphne,
ca. 1470–80, oil on wood,
29.5 x 20 cm, London,
National Gallery, inv. 928.
It was bought in Rome by William
Coningham in 1845, and entered
the National Gallery with the rich
bequest of Wynn Ellis in 1876.
For a long time it was mistakenly
thought to be a decorative
element of a chest.

pl. 23. Piero del Pollaiuolo,
Martyrdom of Saint Sebastian,
1475, oil on wood,
291.5 x 202.6 cm, London,
National Gallery, inv. 292.
The date is recorded by Vasari,
who attributes the altarpiece to
Antonio, contradicted however
by the older sources. It was on
the altar of the Cappella Pucci
in the Santissima Annunziata,
that is, the oratory of Saint
Sebastian adjacent to the
chiostrino dei Voti. Removed
by the Pucci family to their
own palazzo with the excuse
of restoring it, it was sold to
the National Gallery in 1857
by the Marquis Roberto Pucci.

pl. 24. Piero del Pollaiuolo,
Coronation of the Virgin, 1483,
oil on wood, 328 x 242.2 cm,
San Gimignano, Sant'Agostino.
Signed and dated below
"PIERO DEL POLLAIUOLO
FIORENTINO / 1483".
The huge altarpiece was
commissioned by the Augustinian
Domenico Strambi, known as
il dottor parigino (the Parisian
doctor), for the high altar of
the church of Sant'Agostino at
San Gimignano. Removed in the
early nineteenth century to the
collegiate church, it regained
its place in 1937, the year of
its present frame. A careful
restoration performed a few
years ago restored its former
chromatic splendour.

pl. 25. Piero del Pollaiuolo, *Annunciation*, ca. 1480–85, oil on wood, 150.5 x 174.3 cm, Berlin, Staatliche Museen, Gemäldegalerie, inv. 73.
It entered the Berlin museum in 1821 with the rest of the Solly collection, without its provenance being known. The paving with its large marble reflections seems the result of a pentimento, covering an earlier version, with tiny rhomboid and circular decorations that can be glimpsed in transparency.

pl. 26. Piero del Pollaiuolo (?), *Saint Antoninus Worshipping the Crucifix*, 1483, oil and tempera (?) on canvas, 276 x 147 cm, Florence, Museo di San Marco, inv. 277.
Mentioned by Albertini in 1510 as a work by Piero, and ascribed by Vasari to Antonio, the canvas, originally near the tomb of Saint Antoninus, surfaced in 1907 in the convent of San Marco, after centuries of neglect. Ascribed at the time to Baldovinetti, later it was related to Botticini. The detailed sixteenth-century testimony of the Dominican Serafino Razzi strongly indicates Piero for this severely damaged canvas.

pl. 27. Silvestro di Jacopo (Silvestro del Pollaiuolo), *Saint John the Baptist*, ca. 1465–70, pen and black pencil on paper, 27.9 x 19.4 cm, Florence, Galleria degli Uffizi, Gabinetto Disegni e Stampe, inv. 699 E.
Below, in the same ink as the figure, is written the inscription "Saverstro di Jachopo", meant as a signature. Silvestro was the brother of Antonio and Piero, born in ca. 1433. First he was a collaborator in the goldsmith workshop of his older brother, subsequently he appears to have moved to Pisa. That the *Baptist* however is not a work by Antonio, to whom it is usually attributed, is proven by the bristly, quivering sign, so utterly different from the *Adam* [pl. 18].

pl. 28. Antonio del Pollaiuolo, *Funerary Monument to Sixtus IV*, 1484–93, bronze, Vatican City, Basilica di San Pietro, Museo del Tesoro.
On a plate placed behind the head of the deceased we can read: "OPUS ANTONI POLAIOLI / FLORENTINI ARG[ENTO] AUR[O] / PICT[URA] AERE CLARI / AN[NO] DOM[INI]. MCCCCLXXXXIII". It was commissioned by Giuliano Della Rovere, nephew of the pope, immediately following the death of Sixtus IV (12 August 1484). Thus the work took almost ten years. Originally it occupied the centre of the chapel of the Canons' choir, on the south side of the old Saint Peter's.

pl. 29. Antonio del Pollaiuolo, *Justice*, detail of the Funerary Monument to Sixtus IV, 1484–93, bronze, Vatican City, Basilica di San Pietro, Museo del Tesoro.
Often held to be by Piero, the *Virtues* surrounding the pontiff's remains should be given back to Antonio. Removed to the Sacristy during the renovation of the basilica in 1610, the tomb was replaced in Saint Peter's in 1625. In 1922 it was moved to the Museum Petrianum, and then to the Grotte, finally entering the Museo del Tesoro.

pl. 30. Antonio del Pollaiuolo, *Head of Sixtus IV*, detail to the Funerary Monument, 1484–93, bronze, Vatican City, Basilica di San Pietro, Museo del Tesoro.
The Della Rovere emblem appears scores of times on the tomb, concealed among the embroideries of the cushions and the sheet, scattered amidst the allegories of the Arts and Sciences.

pl. 31. Antonio del Pollaiuolo, *Funerary Monument to Innocent VIII*, 1493–97, partially gilded bronze, maximum height (in the present structure) 335 cm, maximum width 238 cm, Vatican City, Basilica di San Pietro.
Commissioned by Lorenzo Cybo, the pope's nephew, originally the monument was backed up to the south pillar of the triumphal arch of the old Constantinian basilica, and the two portraits of Innocent VIII were reversed with respect to the present disposition (alive below, dead above). Dismounted in 1507 to make room for Bramante's new building, it was given the present structure in 1621.

pl. 32. Antonio del Pollaiuolo, *Innocent VIII Blessing*, detail of the *Funerary Monument to Innocent VIII*, ca. 1493–97, partially gilded bronze, Vatican City, Basilica di San Pietro.
The pontiff holds in his left hand the iron of the Holy Lance, that is, the tip of the weapon that was believed to have gone through Christ's side on the day of the Crucifixion. The precious relic had been sent to the pope in 1492, as a diplomatic gift, by the Turkish sultan, Bajazet II. It was kept in a monumental marble ciborium erected in front of the papal tomb.

1

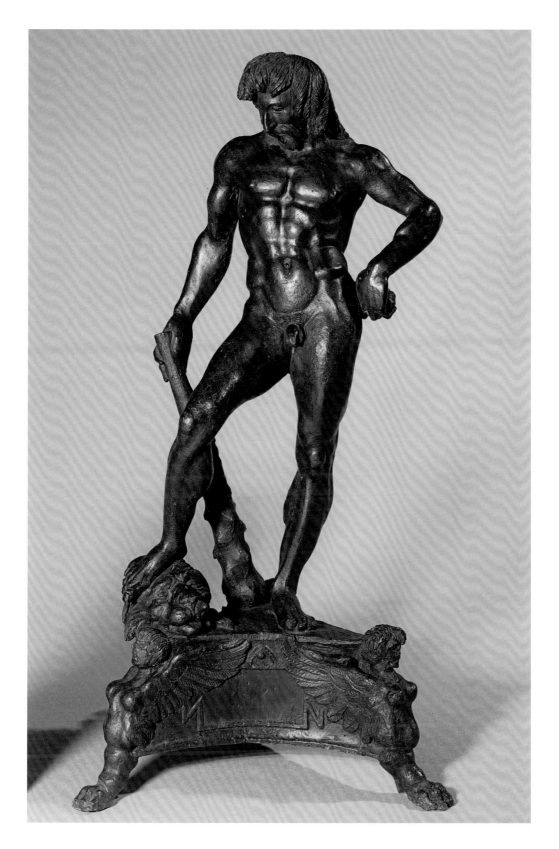

27

APPENDICES

CHRONOLOGY

1431/32
Birth in Florence of Antonio, first son of Jacopo
d'Antonio Benci, poulterer at the Mercato
Vecchio, and his wife Tommasa.

1441/42
Birth of Piero.

1457
30 April: the Arte di Calimala (the wool and
textile guild), in charge of the decoration and
the furnishings of the Florentine baptistery,
resolves to have a large altar cross made in silver
with enamel inlays: the upper part is assigned
to Betto Betti, the base to Antonio [pls. 2, 4]
who, not yet having his own workshop,
is an assistant in Miliano Dei's *bottega*.

1458
28 February: the Operai del Duomo in Florence
commission Antonio to execute two gilt bronze
pyxes (lost).

1459
The cross for the baptistery is completed:
the overall expenditure amounts to 3,036 florins,
of which 2,006 for Antonio and 1,030 for Betto.
On 12 May, before a notary public, Pollaiuolo
becomes independent of his father's
guardianship; that same year leaves the Dei
workshop and enters in partnership with another
goldsmith, Piero di Bartomoleo Sali. In the
autumn he creates a thurible, now lost, for the
Vallombrosan church of San Pancrazio.

1460
The year of the three paintings with the *Labours
of Hercules* for the "Great Hall" of the Palazzo
Medici. In a letter dated 1494, Antonio recalls
having painted them 34 years earlier with one
of his brothers, usually identified with the very
young Piero, although the name of the lesser-
known Silvestro has been suggested. The last to
see and describe the *Labours* was Giorgio Vasari.

1461
3 January: the abbot of San Pancrazio in Florence
asks Antonio and Piero Sali for a silver reliquary
to contain the arm of the titular saint, consigned
several months later (and now lost).
Between January and May the two craftsmen
also receive several payments from the Opera
del Duomo for two silver candelabra,
likewise lost.
7 July: Antonio sells to Cino Rinuccini
a nielloed and fretworked silver buckle
for a woman's belt.

1462
5 April: Antonio is again mentioned in Cino
Rinuccini's diary: he acquires gilt silver chains
for his wife, "per fare fuscoli a campanella"
(for bell-shaped trinkets).
20 July: the Operai of Pistoia Cathedral pay for
two monumental silver and enamel candelabra;
originally commissioned on 5 October from
Piero Sali and Maso Finiguerra, actually Antonio
had a large part in their execution. Dissatisfied
with the fee, Pollaiuolo requested the mediation
of Piero de' Medici, who apparently failed
to obtain an increase in payment.

1464
31 January: Jacopo Baroncelli rented to Antonio
for five years a workshop "actam ad artem
aurificis", which for many years would be
the scene of Antonio's activities. The premises
were in Via Vacchereccia, next to the church of
Santa Cecilia, a stone's throw from the Palazzo
della Signoria. Over the years, associates and
colleagues follow one upon another: for the
period 1464–66 Antonio forms a partnership
with Giuliano di Antonio "et socios", while
his collaboration with Ottaviano, the brother
of the sculptor Agostino di Duccio, lasts until
1471. One of Antonio's brothers, Silvestro, also
belongs to the workshop's team.

1465
This is the year of the commission for two
monumental silver candelabra, almost a metre
and a half tall, that were to accompany the cross

on the baptistery altar: Antonio will complete
them five years later, but they are now lost.
In October Benedetto Salutati buys
silver from "Antonio di Jacopo
and companions, goldsmiths".

1466
In February Antonio is working on enamels
for Benedetto Salutati.
On 17 July he becomes a member of the Arte
della Seta (Silk Guild) in the capacity
of "aurifex aurearius".
In August the embroiderers begin their work
on the parament of Saint John for the Florentine
baptistery: obviously at that date Antonio
had already provided them with the first
designs [pl. 8].
On 1 October he is at Volterra for the restoration
of a silver Madonna in the cathedral, but already
on 20 October, in Florence, he receives 100
florins with his brother Piero "per un lavoro
che tolsono a fare" (for a job they were engaged
to do) in the chapel of the Cardinal of Portugal
at San Miniato al Monte [pl. 9, 10].

1467
1 July: Antonio, Luca della Robbia, and others,
are called upon by the Opera del Duomo
to appraise a large silver cross made by
Bartolomeo di Fruosino for the high altar.
Between November and December he is paid
for the execution of the silver reliquary-bust
of Saint Octavian for the cathedral
of Volterra (lost).
In the course of the year, with his partner
Ottaviano d'Antonio di Duccio, he is paid for
two silver basins for the chapel of the Palazzo
della Signoria: in the fifteen years to come
Pollaiuolo will regularly provide many pieces
in silver for the same chapel, none of which
are identified today.

1468
19 January: Antonio attends the meeting
regarding the question of the metal ball that is
to top the dome of Santa Maria del Fiore: other
craftsmen, such as Luca della Robbia, Mino da

Fiesole and Andrea del Verrocchio, and a number
of important citizens, including the young
Lorenzo de' Medici, are equally present.
On 2 December Pollaiuolo, again along with
Luca and Verrocchio, appraises the copper
"knob" meant to support the ball, made
by Giovanni di Bartomoleo and Bartomoleo
di Fruosino.

1469
1 February: Antonio renews the five-year lease
for the *bottega* in Via Vaccherccia. There, in the
first months of the year, he crafts for Benedetto
Salutati all the parts in precious metals (from
the helmet to the furnishings for the horse, in
gilt silver and enamel) of tournament trappings
that the youth was to wear for the jousting
tournament on Piazza Santa Croce (7 February);
for the same occasion Piero del Pollaiuolo
paints the Salutati standard, representing
a semi-nude nymph.
In June Antonio purchases a large property
at Quarrata, in the *contado* of Pistoia;
on 9 August he is paid for the new designs
for the parament of Saint John.
On 18 August, in the presence of Antonio,
the Università della Mercanzia (Merchants'
Guild) commissions Piero for a panel with the
allegorical figure of *Charity*, to be placed in the
Sala del Consiglio; the work is supervised by the
same Operai who oversee the *Incredulity of Saint
Thomas*, the bronze group assigned to Verrocchio
for the Mercanzia niche at Orsanmichele.
On 18 December Piero delivers the completed
figure, the success of which leads them to
commission him for the six other panels, which
form the complete series of the *Cardinal and
Theological Virtues*. In the course of the year
Antonio was at Spoleto, visiting and bringing
sweetmeats to the elderly Filippo Lippi who,
while still working on frescoes in the cathedral
of the city, dies on 8 October.

1470
2 August: Piero is paid for consigning, with
a significant delay with respect to the contract,
the second and the third figures (*Temperance* and

Faith; pls. 12, 14) for the series for the Mercanzia. On 18 August Sandro Botticelli, who apparently had joined the undertaking, receives the balance for *Fortitude*. In the course of the year Antonio receives the balance due for the two large silver candelabra for the baptistery: in all he receives an unusually high figure of 1,578 florins.

1471

In March Galeazzo Maria Sforza, duke of Milan, is in Florence: on this occasion Piero paints the duke's portrait (now in the Uffizi), which Lorenzo de' Medici kept in his room.

1472

In May Antonio is one of the experts that are to appraise the reliquary of Saint Concordia of the church of San Lorenzo in Florence. On 18 June the Signoria decides to offer Federico da Montefeltro, count of Urbino and recent conqueror of the rebellious Volterra, "un elmetto d'argento, che si fece lavorare da Antonio del Pollajolo" (a silver helmet, crafted by Antonio del Pollaiuolo); on 24 July the master is reimbursed for the silver utilised. Furthermore he is paid for a large silver cup "lavorata chon animali" (crafted with animals), executed for the banker Bartomoleo Cambini. During this year Antonio enrols in the Compagnia di San Luca and, with his brothers Piero and Giovanni, buys a house in Florence, in Piazza degli Agli, in the *popolo* of Santa Maria Maggiore, where the three of them will reside with their respective families.

1473

30 April: Antonio, with other colleagues, appraises the value of the copper "furnishing" executed by the goldsmith Bartomoleo di Fruosino for an antiphonary of the Duomo of Florence. On 23 May Federico da Montefeltro writes to Lorenzo de' Medici greatly praising Antonio, with whom he appears to be acquainted. In August the goldsmith is paid for a silver

cross for the church of the Carmine in Florence, lost long ago.

1474

22 August: Antonio takes legal action against Girolamo Villani, a citizen of Florence, for a debt of eight florins relative to "una cintola d'ariento e più altri arienti a lui dati e venduti" (a silver belt and other silver items delivered and sold to him).

1474–75

Piero paints the *Saint Sebastian* altarpiece [pls. 23] for the Pucci oratory at the Santissima Annunziata (today in London). Vasari (who attributes it to Antonio) claims it "fu finita l'anno 1474" (was completed in 1475), a dating confirmed by two payments in the course of the work, made to Piero in 1474 and recently discovered.

1476

For an unknown patron, Antonio executes the rich sheath for a bread knife, ornamented with elements in enamelled silver, lost.

1477–80

Antonio executes a gilt silver reliquary cross for the monastery of San Gaggio. All that survives are the six enamelled figures, remounted on a sixteenth-century crucifix, today at the Museo Nazionale del Bargello [pl. 21].

1477

11 March: the Operai of the cathedral of San Jacopo at Pistoia write to Lorenzo de' Medici about the monument they intended to have raised to the memory of their fellow-citizen Cardinal Niccolò Forteguerri. Among several models presented a special commission had actually chosen Verrocchio's, but his economic claims exceeded the sum set by the Pistoiese. So the people in charge, "intendendo essere qui Piero del Pollaiuolo" (having heard Piero del Pollaiuolo was here), had addressed him for another model which, when consigned, had seemed to them "più bello e più degno d'arte" (more beautiful

and worthy of art). Since Verrocchio nonetheless protested, backed by the Florentine *Commissari* (board members) in Pistoia, the Operai turn to the Magnifico for his opinion, "perché di simili cose e d'ogni altra n'avete pienissima intelligentia" (since you have complete understanding of these matters and all others). Finally the commission would be awarded to Verrocchio.

24 July: in Florence the glorious silver frontal of the baptistery altar, begun in the fourteenth century, is to be completed with two sidepieces. On 2 August Andrea del Verrocchio and Antonio del Pollaiuolo are paid for several models related to this project, two weeks later Bernardo Cennini and the firm formed by Antonio di Salvi and Francesco di Giovanni are also involved in the task.

11 September: in his book of *Ricordanze* (*Recollections*), Antonio Rospigliosi, Antonio and Piero's legal representative at Pistoia, notes he leased for three years a farm in the *comune di Quarrata*, "la quale terra aviamo tolta per Jacopo del Polaiuolo di Firenze, a' prieghi di Piero suo figliuolo" (the land we took for Jacopo del Pollaiuolo in Florence at the request of his son Piero). At the term of the contract the farm was purchased by Antonio.

19 November: Antonio forms a company with the young Paolo di Giovanni Sogliani, born in 1455, a distant cousin of the more renowned painter Giovannantonio; the firm will last ten years and Sogliani will continue to run it after Pollaiuolo's removal to Rome. In the course of the year the workshop produces a silver cross commissioned by Fra Michele Cambini, of the Santa Croce monastery, of which we know nothing further.

24 December: Piero receives from the Signoria the assignment to paint an altarpiece for the chapel of San Bernardo in Palazzo Vecchio; however the commission is cancelled a few days later and first transferred to Leonardo, then to Ghirlandaio, without ever being carried out.

1478

The work on the reliefs of the silver altar with the *Stories of the Baptist* is protracted: on 13 January the tasks are redistributed among the four workshops involved, setting the final date to 20 July, but still on 30 December neither Antonio nor Verrocchio have delivered the work, so they are solicited once again by the Arte di Calamala.

13 April: the Operai del Duomo of Florence commission to Antonio, for the price of 30 gold florins, a reliquary for the finger of Saint John the Baptist, for which he receives an advance on 27 December (this work is also lost). In the course of the year Antonio works also on a purse "con fornimento d'oro" (with gold ornaments) for Cardinal Francesco Gonzaga.

1479

19 July: Antonio Rospigliosi notes in his *Ricordanze* having paid, on the account of Antonio, who commits himself to pay him back, for a "giovencho di cinque anni" (five year-old ox).

1480

Antonio and Piero register their tax returns to the land office. "Antonio di Jachopo, horafo del pollaiuolo" (Antonio di Jacopo, goldsmith son of the poulterer), forty-nine years old and married to one Marietta twenty years his younger, claims the house in Piazza degli Agli, land and houses in the area of Quarrata, a holding in Florence, beyond the Porta al Prato. He practises his profession in the workshop in Via Vacchereccia with his partner Paolo Sogliani. Piero, 33 years old, aside from the house shared with his brother, declares he leases a farm in the Pistoia region and a small house in Florence that he uses as a workshop for his craft as a painter. During the year the balance for the silver panel with the *Nativity of Saint John* for the altar of the baptistery is finally recorded, paid to Antonio and his partner 487 florins, 1 *lira*, 16 *soldi* and 4 *denari*.

1481

17 February: Antonio is at San Gimignano with another goldsmith, Antonio di Salvi, to appraise a reliquary executed by a certain Jacopo da Pisa; during the year he buys a house in Florence.

1482

19 August: Antonio is paid for a silver "rinfreschatoio" (cooler) for the Palazzo della Signoria, while in October Piero is engaged to paint one of the walls of the Sala dei Signori (today Sala dei Gigli), but the project will not be carried out.

2 December: Antonio Rospigliosi notes in his book of *Ricordanze* having leased for five years, for the benefit of Piero del Pollaiuolo, a large property at Buriano, in the Pistoiese *contado*, with a house, farmyard, oven, coppice and woods: standing surety for Piero is Giovanni Lanfredini, who sent a letter to that effect to Rospigliosi from Florence. Even before the contract expires, 18 November 1485, Piero would buy that piece of property. The same year a letter was addressed from Marsilio Ficino to the Venetian Pietro Molin, in which he mentions "Antonius noster, pictor et sculptor insignis".

1483

The year is marked by the altarpiece on the high altar of Sant'Agostino at San Gimignano [pl. 24], signed by Pietro. According to the sixteenth-century chronicle by Serafino Razzi, the prior of the convent of San Marco in Florence, Francesco Salviati, commissioned to "Pollaiuolo florentine painter" the large canvas with *Saint Antoninus Worshipping the Crucifix* [pl. 26].

26 April: Antonio, with Verrocchio and Bernardo Cennini, received a payment "per rassettare … le storie che feciono nell'altare di S. Giovanni" (to mend … the *storie* appearing on the altar of Saint John).

1484

28 May: Giovanni Lanfredini, from Naples (where he had recently been appointed ambassador to the Florentines), writes to Antonio in Florence, glorifying Rome and inviting him to come to the pontifical city. The guest must have soon been welcomed, since on 11 and 20 August Antonio's young associate Paolo Sogliani, claims, in joining the Arte della Seta, that he is waiting for Antonio to return from Rome. So Pollaiuolo moved some time between June and early August, when the commission for the tomb of Sixtus IV (deceased 12 August) must have been issued on behalf of Cardinal Giuliano Della Rovere.

1485

Antonio is back in Florence, where he collects rent from houses he owns on 27 August and 7 September.

11 November: the *Comune di Pistoia* urges the Compagnia di San Zenone to pay for the panel "of the corpus domini" for the cathedral, commissioned some time before to Piero del Pollaiuolo and that the painter had already executed and delivered; a week later, on the 18 November, Piero finally receives the balance for his work and immediately invests the money in buying a farm at Buriano. This is the last document relating to his lifetime.

1486

28 November: Antonio is indebted to Francesco Bonaparte for the purchase of several precious stones.

1489

12 November: Lorenzo il Magnifico writes to Giovanni Lanfredini, the Medicean agent at the Holy See, a letter in which he refers very mysteriously to certain affairs about which he talked to Pollaiuolo "in questa tornata in costà di Antonio" (during one of Antonio's stays in Florence).

1491

5 January: Antonio's name appears among those of the masters who presented a design for the new facade of Santa Maria del Fiore. 27 July in the registers of Lorenzo il Magnifico's correspondence a letter to "Antonio del Pollaiuolo, risposta ad una sua" (Antonio del Pollaiuolo, reply to his) is recorded.

1492

4 February: the registers of Lorenzo's correspondence mention a letter "to monsignor

Ascanio [Sforza] for Antonio del Pollaiuolo".
On 8 April il Magnifico dies: the inventory
of the Palazzo Medici drafted on the occasion
mentions, aside from the three Hercules
paintings, a bronze with Hercules and Antaeus
by Antonio (today in the Bargello; pl. 17)
and the portrait of Galeazzo Maria Sforza
by Piero (in the Uffizi).
Apparently during the year Antonio presented
a design for the construction of the church
of Santa Maria dell'Umiltà at Pistoia.

1493
This is the year inscribed on the Funerary
Monument to Sixtus IV in the Vatican
[pls. 28, 30].
27 August: Antonio prepares to return to Florence
"per alqune sue occurrentie ... et recuperazione
dele sue cose" (for some business ... and to
recover some of his possessions); on the occasion
Cardinal Giuliano Della Rovere writes for him
a letter of recommendation addressed to Piero
di Lorenzo de' Medici.

1494
13 July: Antonio writes to Gentil Virginio Orsini
asking him to recommend him to Piero de'
Medici: in fact he hopes to obtain an
authorisation to visit his holdings between
Quarrata and Poggio a Caiano, a dispensation
of the prohibition to travel imposed owing
to the current plague. In the letter, which also
mentions the *Labours of Hercules* for the Palazzo
Medici, painted 34 years earlier, Pollaiuolo also
proposes to Orsini to do his portrait in bronze.

1495
On 26 March and 6 April Antonio buys
other land in the Quarrata area. On 20 May
he presents to the Operai di Santo
Spirito in Florence a model for the dome
to be built for their sacristy. On 8 August
the Pistoiese architect Ventura Vitoni comes
to Florence to discuss the construction of the
church of Santa Maria dell'Umiltà in Pistoia:
he meets Antonio del Pollaiuolo and Antonio
da Sangallo. Other contacts between the three

of them are regularly attested throughout the
month of October.

1496
4 November: Antonio, in Rome, writes his will,
from which we find out among other things that
he has two daughters, Marietta and Maddalena,
born of his second wife, Lucrezia Fantoni; we
also learn that Piero had died in the meantime.

1498
On 30 January the remains of Innocent VIII are
removed to the Funerary Monument decorated
by Antonio in Saint Peter's [pls. 31, 32].
4 February: the artist dies in Rome and is
buried in San Pietro in Vincoli. Ten days later
the Signoria of Florence writes to its ambassador
in Rome, Domenico Bonsi, instructing him to
pay the balance due to the widow of Antonio,
"sculptore celeberrimo" (most famous sculptor),
creditor of the cardinals Lorenzo Cybo and
Ascanio Sforza, "per certe cose a loro lavorate
di suo magisterio" (for certain articles crafted
for them under his direction). A very warm
request "essendo stato dicto Antonio nostro
cittadino e huomo unico nella arte sua"
(Antonio being our citizen and unique in his art).

CONTEMPORARIES

The names of the two Pollaiuolo (more often Antonio's) frequently appear in texts by their contemporaries. Among the citations in diaries, recollections, estate inventories there is the special case of the *Libro d'inventario dei beni di Lorenzo il Magnifico* (edited by M. Spallanzani and G. Gaeta Bertelà, Florence: S.P.E.S., 1992), that mentions the presence of Pollaiuolesque sculptures and paintings in several rooms of Palazzo Medici. However, the two brothers' intellectual standing is reflected in other quotations, more precisely literary and celebrative in tenor, to begin with that by Filarete who, already in the early fourteen-sixties, named Antonio as one of the goldsmiths it would have been good to involve in the project for Filarete's imaginary city, the Sforzinda: (Antonio Averlino, called Filarete, *Trattato di architettura*, edited by A. M. Finoli and L. Grassi, 2 vols., Milan: Il Polifilo, 1972, I, p. 251). Then Ugolino Verino (Florence, 1438–1516), inclined to glorify painters and sculptors in verse, wrote at length on the Pollaiuolo. In the first version of his *Carliade*, a poem narrating the exploits of Charlemagne on the model of the *Aeneid*, he introduced as frescoing the imaginary walls of a prince's palace, Sandro Botticelli and one of the Pollaiuolo, although it is not clear which of the two brothers is concealed under the classic identity of "Pullus Thyrrenus" (Ugolino Verino, *Carlias: ein Epos des 15. Jahrhunderts*, edited by N. Thurn, Munich: Fink, 1995). Soon Antonio and Piero appear again as a pair in the epigram *De pictoribus et scultoribus florentinis qui priscis graecis equiperari possunt* (Book III, 23: published a number of times, cf. now in U. Verino, *Epigrammi*, edited by F. Bausi, Messina: Sicania, 1998, pp. 324–28 and 571), and finally once again in the *De illustratione urbis Florentiae* (Ugolinus Virinus, *De illustratione urbis Florentiae*. Paris: Mamert Patisson, 1583, p. 13). Mandatory on Ugolino Verino and

the artists the reference to E. H. Gombrich, "Apollonio di Giovanni. A Florentine Cassone Workshop seen through the Eyes of a Humanist Poet", *Journal of the Warburg and Courtauld Institutes*, XVIII, 1955, pp. 16–34 (then in *Norm and Form. Studies in the Art of the Renaissance*, London: Phaidon, 1966). The consideration in which the Florentine humanist circles hold the Pollaiuolo is also confirmed by letters, such as the one, perhaps written in 1477, from Antonio Ivani, chancellor of the Florentines at Pistoia, to Marsilio Ficino (praising "Petrum Pollariolum alterum Prasitelem", to whom we hear Ficino is "vehementissime affectum"); or the other, also from Marsilio, to the Venetian Pietro Molin in 1482 (for both: A. Chastel, *Marsile Ficin et l'art*, Geneva: Droz, 1954, pp. 32, 38 notes 63–65, and cf. also pp. 195–96). Very soon Antonio's name echoes beyond Florence as well and, even before praise for the pontifical bronzes resounds in Rome, his fame reaches Urbino, where Federico da Montefeltro is devoted to him (A. Parronchi, "Prima traccia dell'attività del Pollaiolo per Urbino", *Studi urbinati di storia, filosofia e letteratura*, XLV, 1971, pp. 1176–93) and Giovanni Santi acclaims his triumphal helmet (G. Santi, *La vita e le gesta di Federico da Montefeltro, duca d'Urbino*, edited by L. Michelini Tocci, 2 vols., Vatican City: Biblioteca Apostolica Vaticana, 1985, vol. II, pp. 406, 674). Toward the end of the century, "Prospectivo Melanese" in the *Antiquarie prospetiche Romane* is the most inspired eulogist of pope Sixtus IV's tomb, edited by Giovanni Agosti and Dante Isella (Parma: Guanda, 2004, pp. 26, 120–2).

FROM THE SIXTEENTH CENTURY TO NEOCLASSICISM

In order to comprehend relations between the two brothers and clearly distinguish their catalogues, the writers on art preceding Vasari are essential, above all Francesco Albertini, *Memoriale di molte statue et picture sono nella inclyta ciptà di Florentia per mano di sculptori et pictori excellenti, moderni et antiqui*, ser Antonio Tubini, Florence: 1510 (facsimile ed. included in *Five Early Guides* to *Rome and Florence*, edited by P. Murray, Farnborough: Gregg, 1972); then *Il Libro di Antonio Billi* (ca. 1506–30: *Il Libro di Antonio Billi*, edited by C. Frey, Berlin: Grote, 1892; 2nd ed. by F. Benedettucci. Anzio: De Rubeis, 1991); and last, the Anonimo Magliabechiano (ca. 1540–45: *Il codice magliabechiano cl. XVII.17 contenente notizie sopra l'arte degli Antichi e quella de' Fiorentini da Cimabue a Michelangelo Buonarroti*, edited by C. Frey, Berlin: Grote, 1892, p. 81; more recently: *L'Anonimo Magliabechiano*, edited by A. Ficarra, Naples: Fiorentino, 1968). The double biography by Vasari, scarcely altered between the first edition (1550) and the second (1568), resumes all the earlier indications, but arranges them in view of a far greater literary ambition, and while it is mistaken in concentrating entirely on the figure of Antonio, obfuscating his brother, it focuses nonetheless on the outstanding traits of the Pollaiuolesque aesthetics that the successive literature would crystallise into a formula: incisiveness of draughtsmanship, exceptional anatomical competence, but also peculiarity of the oil colouring (G. Vasari, *Le vite de' più eccellenti pittori, scultori e architettori*, in the 1550 and 1568 versions, edited by R. Bettarini and P. Barocchi, 6 vols., Florence: Sansoni, then S.P.E.S., 1966–87, vol. III, 1971, pp. 499–508). Vasari's point of view influences most of the later bibliography, which is often a mere echo of Vasari, from Raffaello Borghini (*Il Riposo*, Florence: Giorgio Marescotti, 1584, pp. 348–50) to Francesco Bocchi (*Le bellezze della città di Fiorenza*, Florence: Bartolomeo Sermartelli, 1591, pp. 196, 205; facsimile ed. Bologna: Forni, 1974), up to Filippo Baldinucci (*Notizie de' professori del disegno da Cimabue in qua*, 6 vols., Florence: various pubs., 1681–1728; III, 1728, posthumous, pp. 116–18); the late eighteenth century follows suit with Luigi Lanzi (*Storia pittorica della Italia*, 3 vols., Bassano: Remondini, 1795–96, vol. I, p. 67), in which special praise is given to the etching with the *Battle of the Ten Nudes*. On the other hand, Cicognara's idolatry for Canova explains his preference for the "elegant simplicity" of the monument to Innocent VIII over the excessive

ornamentation of the one for Sixtus IV (L. Cicognara, *Storia della scultura in Italia dal suo risorgimento sino al secolo di Napoleone*, 3 vols., Venice: Picotti, 1813–18, I, p. 123). In this context Benvenuto Cellini's praise in his treatise on goldwork stands out as entirely original and independent (1568: cf. the classic edition by C. Milanesi, *I Trattati dell'Oreficeria e della Scultura di Benvenuto Cellini novamente messi alle stampe secondo la originale dettatura del codice marciano*, Florence: Le Monnier, 1857, p. 7; now republished in B. Cellini, *Dell'oreficeria*, edited by A. Capitano, Turin: Nino Aragno, 2002): as opposed to Vasari's insistence on Antonio as a painter, Cellini makes clear that: "he was a goldsmith, and was so great a draughtsman […] that many sculptors and painters, I'm speaking of the greatest in these arts, still use his drawings […] The man did but few other things, but only drew admirably, and always attained that great draughtsmanship".

DOCUMENTS

Archive research takes on a very special meaning in the case of Antonio Pollaiuolo, raising the memory, almost the ghost, of several major goldworks, as well as endless reliquaries and crosses and enamels, all of which are lost, yet that must have been the artist's daily practice. We can look all the way back to Vincenzo Borghini's investigations on the tournament trappings the two Pollaiuolo made for Benedetto Salutati (Vincenzo Borghini, *Discorsi*, 2 vols., Florence: Giunti, 1584–85, vol. II, pp. 162–64); a hundred years later Baldinucci pointed out the commission for the helmet for Montefeltro (F. Baldinucci, *Notizie de' professori…*, op. cit.) and protracted rummaging amidst the papers went on in the eighteenth century with details on the silver altar of the Baptistery contributed by Anton Francesco Gori (*Monumenta sacrae vetustatis insigniae Baptisteri Florentini*, Florence: Albizzini, 1756) and Giuseppe Richa (*Notizie istoriche delle chiese fiorentine divise ne' suoi quartieri*, 10 vols., Florence: Viviani, 1754–62;

vol. IV, p. 71; vol. VI, pp. 188, 367; vol. VIII, p. 54; vol. X, pp. 355–56. facsimile ed., Rome: Multigrafica, 1989). Yet understandably it was the nineteenth century that would provide the most conspicuous results: a great deal of material in G. Gaye, *Carteggio inedito d'artisti dei secoli XIV-XVII*, 3 vols., Florence: Molini, 1839–40, vol. I, pp. 265–66, 340–41, 570–71; vol. II, p. 470; for Antonio's Roman testament in 1498, see M. Gualandi, *Memorie originali italiane risguardanti le belle arti*, s. V, Bologna: Tipografia sassi nelle Spaderie, 1844, no. 155, pp. 39–50. Then in 1849 the fifth volume of the Le Monnier edition of Vasari's *Vite* appeared (G. Vasari, *Le vite de' più eccellenti pittori, scultori e architetti*, edited by the "Società di amatori delle Arti belle" [V. Marchese, C. Pini, C., and G. Milanesi], 13 vols., Florence: Le Monnier, 1846–57, vol. V, pp. 90–109) with the usual flood of information concealed in the notes, developed and enriched by Gaetano Milanesi alone in the successive Sansoni edition (*Le Vite de' più eccellenti pittori, scultori ed architettori*, with new annotations and commentaries by G. Milanesi, 6 vols., Florence: Sansoni, 1878–81, vol. III, pp. 285–307). At the end of the century, in an unusual context, the letter written in 1494 by the elderly Antonio to Virginio Orsini was printed (L. Borsari, *Lettera di Antonio del Pollajuolo*, gift for the Orsini-Varo wedding), Rome: 1891; see the commentary by A. Venturi, *Archivio storico dell'arte*, V, 1892, pp. 208–10, and the more accessible re-edition, with several corrections, by J. Del Badia, "Lettera d'Antonio del Pollaiuolo a Virgilio Orsini del 14 luglio 1494", *Rivista d'arte*, III, 1905, pp. 125–26). Archive investigations continued to swell in the early twentieth century: A. Chiti, "Di una tavola ignota di Piero del Pollaiuolo", *Bollettino storico pistoiese*, II, 1900, pp. 41–48; J. Mesnil, "Botticelli, les Pollaiuoli et Verrocchio", *Rivista d'arte*, III, 1905, pp. 4–12; M. Cruttwell, "Quattro portate del catasto e della decima fatte da Antonio Pollajuolo, dal fratello Giovanni e da Jacopo loro padre", *L'Arte*, VIII, 1905, pp. 381–85; O. Giglioli, "Antonio Pollaiuolo proprietario di case", *Illustratore fiorentino*, IV, 1907, pp. 77–78; *Libro A di richordi d'Antonio di*

Taddeo Rospiglioxi (1459–1498), with a dedicatory letter by G. C. Rospigliosi, preface and index by L. Andreani, Pisa: Mariotti, 1909 (with much information, still barely explored, on the presence of Antonio and Piero at Pistoia); L. Fausti, "Le pitture di Fra Filippo Lippi nel Duomo di Spoleto", *Archivio per la storia ecclesiastica dell'Umbria*, II, 1915 (with the document attesting Antonio's presence at Spoleto in 1469); E. Wilder (text), P. Bacci (documents), C. Kennedy (photographs), *The Unfinished Monument by Andrea del Verrocchio to the Cardinal Niccolò Forteguerri at Pistoia*, Northampton, Mass.–Florence: Smith College-Tyszkiewicz, 1932 (on Piero's share in the work). After the last world war, still regarding documents, we should mention the discoveries of R. G. Mather ("Documents mostly new relating to Florentine Painters and Sculptors of the Fifteenth Century", *Art Bulletin*, XXX, 1948, pp. 20–65: for the two Pollaiuolo, pp. 32–35); the edition of the *Protocolli del carteggio di Lorenzo il Magnifico per gli anni 1473–74, 1477–92*, edited by M. Del Piazzo, Florence: L. S. Olschki, 1956, pp. 466, 486 (revealing the existence of two lost letters from Lorenzo concerning Antonio del Pollaiuolo); the above-mentioned Urbino disclosure by Alessandro Parronchi; the profitable specification by E. Borsook ("Two Letters concerning Antonio Pollaiuolo", *The Burlington Magazine*, CXV, 844, 1973, pp. 464–68: reassigns to its true author Jacopo Lanfredini the letter in which Antonio del Pollaiuolo is glorified as "el principale maestro di questa città", until then attributed to Lorenzo il Magnifico). More recently there has been a surge in investigations into the complex network of societies and companies Antonio set up with other goldsmiths: M. Haines, "Documenti intorno al Reliquiario di San Pancrazio di Antonio Pollaiolo e Piero Sali", in *Scritti di storia dell'arte in onore di Ugo Procacci*, 2 vols., Milan: Electa, 1977, vol. II, pp. 264–69; D. Liscia Bemporad, "Appunti sulla bottega orafa di Antonio del Pollaiolo e di alcuni suoi allievi", *Antichità viva*, XIX, 3, 1980, pp. 47–53; D. Carl, "Zur Goldschmiedefamilie Die, mit neuen

Dokumenten zu Antonio Pollaiuolo und Andrea Verrocchio", *Mitteilungen des Kunsthistorischen Institutes in Florenz*, XXVI, 1982, pp. 129–66; Eadem, "Addenda zu Antonio Pollaiuolo und seiner Werkstatt", *Mitteilungen des Kunsthistorischen Institutes in Florenz*, XXVII, 1983, pp. 285–306; L. Melli, "Antonio del Pollaiolo orafo e la sua bottega 'magnifica ed onorata in Mercato Nuovo'", *Prospettiva*, 109, 2003, pp. 65–75. Among the dozens of Pollaiuolo's more or less well-known colleagues, Ottaviano d'Antonio di Duccio, brother of the sculptor Agostino di Duccio, stands out: all the works created in collaboration are lost, but their relationship is reflected in the only ascertained work by Ottaviano, the tomb of the bishop Antonio Malatesta da Fossombrone in the cathedral of Cesena (1467), with two tapering angels, rather ugly but entirely Pollaiuolesque. See also several documents relative to a bronze angel for the cathedral of Pisa, designed by "Ottaviano di Antonio da Firenze, compagno d'Antonio del Pollaiuolo" (I. B. Supino, *I pittori e gli scultori del Rinascimento nella primaziale di Pisa*, Rome: Unione cooperativa editrice, 1894, p. 11; R. P. Ciardi, *Il Quattrocento*, in R. P. Ciardi, C. Casini and L. Tongiorgi Tomasi, *Scultura a Pisa tra Quattro e Seicento*, Pisa: Cassa di Risparmio, 1987, pp. 12–110, in particular pp. 75, 108, note 159).

FROM CAVALCASELLE TO BERENSON

Cavalcaselle and Crowe in their *New History* took the first steps toward a complete reinterpretation of the personalities of the two Pollaiuolo brothers, supported by discoveries made in the archives, at last drawing art literature out of the shallows in which, over-confident in Vasari's compass, it had run aground: J. A. Crowe, G. B. Cavalcaselle, *A New History of Painting in Italy from the Second to the Sixteenth Century*, 3 vols., London: Murray, 1864–66, vol. II, pp. 382–99, 413. The most striking point in the interpretation of Cavalcaselle, who does not display much enthusiasm for the two Pollaiuolo (as will later

be the case with Longhi), is the accurate link established between Antonio's pictorial style and the practice of goldwork, even though it leads to a negative judgement for the excessively detailed and angular forms deriving from it in the paintings, and for their bronze-like, oil-saturated colouring, resembling translucent varnish. But even more remarkable is the distinction Cavalcaselle makes among the corpus of paintings made between works he considers have a greater plastic incisiveness—and therefore ascribable to Antonio—and those in which he believes a truly pictorial conception prevails (Berlin *Annunciation*, Turin *Archangel Raphael and Tobias*, London *Saint Sebastian*), which should therefore be attributed to Piero; these conclusions are endorsed by information given by Albertini (the only one of Vasari's sources published at the time). A similar point of view is further developed in the pioneering essay by H. Ulmann, "Bilder und Zeichnungen der Brüder Pollajuoli", *Jahrbuch der königlich preußischen Kunstsammlungen*, XV, 1894, pp. 230–47, which is also important for the pointed reinterpretation of the available documents, though impaired by a series of rash attributions, a fact that caused Ulmann's essay to be too hastily forgotten. Bernard Berenson's point of view is completely different. He is Antonio's most fervent champion, and places him at the apex of his personal vision of the Florentine Renaissance. Ever since the first edition of the *Florentine Painters* (B. Berenson, *The Florentine Painters of the Renaissance*, New York-London: Putnam's, 1896, pp. 125–26) we can see Berenson's favour for the elder as responsible for the principal paintings, in particular the large altarpiece with the *Saint Sebastian*, whereas he proposes that Piero "worked mainly to his brother's designs". The opportunity for a thorough reappraisal of the brothers' work appears a few years later (B. Berenson, *The Drawings of the Florentine Painters*, 2 vols., London: Murray, 1903, vol. I, pp. 17–31), in which the author deals essentially with paring down a catalogue that had become inflated with false attributions, while carefully redistributing the works between Antonio and Piero, bearing in mind that Piero is a painter "of unalloyed mediocrity, with scarcely a touch of charm to repay the absence of life and vigour", whereas Antonio is "one of the ablest interpreters of the human body as a vehicle of life, communicating energy and exulting power". And in describing the etching with the *Battle of the Ten Nudes* Berenson provides its most cogent characterisation: "The pleasure we take in these savagely battling forms arises from their power to directly communicate life, to immensely heighten our sense of vitality. .... See how the prostrate man plants his foot on the thigh of his enemy, and note the tremendous energy he exerts to keep off the foe. ... We imagine ourselves imitating all of the movements, and exerting the force required of them. ... And thus while under the spell of the illusion—this hyperaesthesia not brought with drugs, and not paid for with cheques drawn on our vitality— we feel as if the elixir of life, not our own sluggish blood, were coursing through our veins": we feel like we are watching a *Fight Club* scene.

FROM BERENSON TO LONGHI

Although partial and somewhat distorted, the interpretation Berenson offered was fascinating, and met with immediate and lasting success. In particular, Maud Cruttwell followed in Berenson's wake with her book *Antonio Pollaiuolo* (London-New York: Scribner's, 1907), the first monograph on both brothers, even though, significantly, the book title carried Antonio's name alone. It is a refreshing, pleasant book, brought up to date with the many discoveries that had enriched the Pollaiuolo catalogue between the late nineteenth and the early twentieth centuries; as early as 1880 Giovanni Morelli had in fact reassigned to Antonio several of his most important drawings (J. Lermolieff, *Le opere dei maestri italiani nelle Gallerie di Monaco, Dresda e Berlino*, Bologna: Zanichelli, 1886, pp. 85–92: Munich, design for an equestrian monument to Francesco Sforza; Idem, *Die Galerien Borghese und Doria Panfili in Rom*, Leipzig: Brockhaus, 1890, p. 119: *Adam and Eve* of the Uffizi); in 1897 Mary Logan published the mural painting that had been discovered under the plaster at the Villa La Gallina in Arcetri (M. Logan, "Découverte d'une fresque de Pollaiolo", *Chronique des Arts*, 1897, pp. 343–44); eight years later Berenson himself brought to light the Staggia altarpiece (B. Berenson, "Due quadri inediti a Staggia", *Rassegna d'arte*, V, 1905, pp. 9–11), and meanwhile the shield with *Milon of Croton* and the small panel with *Hercules, Nessus and Deianeira* had come to light (the first at the sale of the Capel Cure collection: C. J. Ffoulkes, "Notizie d'Inghilterra. Vendite della primavera", *L'Arte*, VIII, 1905, pp. 283–88; the second in the Jarves collection: F. J. Mather, "The New Haven Pollaiuolo", *The Burlington Magazine*, VIII, 1905–06, pp. 440–43). Cruttwell's book was severely criticised by Wilhelm Bode ("A new book on the Pollaiuoli", *The Burlington Magazine*, XI, 1907, pp. 181–82), who accused the author of being a dilettante and of blindly adhering to Berenson's position (Berenson being the real target of his polemic); this time, however, the legendary director of the Kaiser Friedrich Museum of Berlin missed his target (and betrayed a strong vein of misogyny) particularly as the most serious error imputed to Cruttwell was to have attributed to Antonio Pollaiuolo the profile painting in the Museo Poldi Pezzoli in Milan (which for Bode was the work of Domenico Veneziano). The rather uneventful panorama of successive studies on the Pollaiuolo has made today's critics more indulgent, and, although obviously now out of date, Cruttwell's book of 1907 remains one of the most appealing of the monographs devoted to the brothers. For Adolfo Venturi (*Storia dell'arte italiana. La scultura del Quattrocento*, vol. VI, Milan: Ulrico Hoepli, 1908, pp. 734–47) "Antonio Pollaiuolo is a peasant decked out in embroidered clothes, whose behaviour is violent despite his fancy costume, and who with big limbs and knotty fingers and iron sinews rends bejewelled cloaks"; the two Roman tombs are elegantly described, yet with some reserves on the allegories of Sixtus's tomb ("they are not appealing figures, especially when expressing ecstasy or admiration"). Three years later, in

Venturi's book on painting (*Storia dell'arte italiana. La Pittura del Quattrocento*, vol. VII.1, Milan: Ulrico Hoepli, 1911, pp. 558–78), the echo of Berenson vividly resounds once again: "rendering the athletic form in a supreme muscular effort, in a heroic violence, was Antonio's aim … the rough plastic energy of Andrea del Castagno reached its apotheosis in the Pollaiuolo". Venturi will come back again to the pontifical bronzes, but much later (*Storia dell'arte italiana. L'architettura del Quattrocento*, vol. VIII.1, Milan: Ulrico Hoepli, 1923, pp. 641–49) and, almost as though wishing to correct himself, he invents a highly expressive and now entirely positive interpretation: "The angular, broken, swift outline acquires energetic value … the surfaces constantly ripple, break, and vary; the complex faceting of the wedge-shaped forms, with prismatic hollows, contribute a pictorial mobility of reflections and shadows; release bronze sparks". However his interpretation of the tomb of Innocent VIII in pre-Baroque terms is not convincing.

Someone who definitely could have outmoded the Berensonian approach was Roberto Longhi, and while the Pollaiuolo brothers were far from being his favourites, on at least a couple of occasions he hints at a very different interpretation. In 1925 (R. Longhi, "Un frammento della pala di Domenico Veneziano per Santa Lucia de' Magnoli", *L'arte*, XXVIII, 1925, pp. 31–35 [now in *Saggi e ricerche, 1925–1928*, edition of the complete works of R. Longhi, vol. II, Sansoni, Florence: 1967, pp. 3–8]), openly lashing out against the Donatello-Andrea del Castagno genealogy, which was always given as the source of the Pollaiuolesque style, Longhi forcefully introduces the precedent of Domenico Veneziano, and claims for the paintings of the two brothers (here still undistinguished) an authentic pictorial quality that had been negated by the graphic-anatomical insistence of Berenson's interpretation, even comparing the landscapes to the supreme ones of Van Eyck: "In any case we should look to Veneziano for all the intimately pictorial qualities that make us look at the Pollaiuolo very differently than we did in the days

when the critics were used to the functional line. Today who can fail to see that the landscape beyond the window of the Berlin *Annunciation* does not lose its substantial impressionism, not even after then looking straight away at the *Baptism of Christ* in the Milan *Hours*? Or after opening the window of the *Annunciation* in the Ghent panels?". After over a quarter of a century, in the last lines of the famous essay on the Master of Pratovecchio (R. Longhi, "Il "Maestro di Pratovecchio"", *Paragone*, 35, 1952, pp. 10–37; now in *"Fatti di Masolino e di Masaccio" e altri studi sul Quattrocento, 1910–1967*, edition of the complete works of R. Longhi, vol. VIII.1, Florence: Sansoni, 1975, pp. 99–122, p. 115), the two Pollaiuolo have become the most legitimate heirs of the great anonymous artist's lesson; and this time their personalities are sharply distinct: "Precisely the two consecutive aspects of the 'Maestro di Pratovecchio', the brightness of a flowery world, and then mobile, mournful energy, are reflected, the former in Piero Pollaiuolo (anyone examining the three Saints of San Miniato, dated 1467, will be instantly convinced), the latter in Antonio." But Longhi was not without reserve: "Had he not subsequently forgotten that, in the beautiful days, the movements of the body were supposed to reflect those of the soul, something that solicits, almost more than artistic judgement, moral judgement."

ITALIAN MONOGRAPHS

In the 1940s Italy saw a surge of Pollaiuolesque studies, with the appearance of three new monographs. The first is the elegant book by G. Colacicchi, *Antonio del Pollaiuolo*, (Florence: Chessa, 1943), with a wordy, indigestible essay, stamped with the most anti-historical formalism, where for pages and pages Pollaiuolo's name is not even mentioned, lost while the author rambles on about Byzantine painting, Giotto, and Michelangelo. Very different the style of A. Sabatini, *Antonio e Piero del Pollaiolo* (Florence: Sansoni, 1944), a somewhat scanty edition published during the war, with a handful of inferior reproductions. Sabatini's doctoral thesis was published posthumously (with a brief recollection of the author by Mario Salmi on p. 139); accompanying the very diligent essay, the rigorous appendices continue to be immensely useful, with their trove of biographical data, catalogue of works, and history. This vital information used extensively by S. Ortolani, *Il Pollaiuolo* (Milan: Ulrico Hoepli, 1948), though the result is pretentious, and spoiled by rhetorical outbursts, and repeated diversions; however, the first-rate repertory of illustrations also covers several problematic and less-known works. Then in Italy a silence of almost forty years fell on the two Pollaiuolo, interrupted by the entries compiled by Marco Chiarini ("Benci, Antonio" and "Benci, Piero") for the *Dizionario Biografico degli Italiani*, vol. VIII, 1966, pp. 183–89, 197–200; and the not very useful A. Busignani, *Pollaiolo* in the *I più eccellenti* series (Florence: Il Fiorino, 1969).

THE LAST THIRTY YEARS

There is no lack of good ideas in the monograph by L. D. Ettlinger, *Antonio and Piero Pollaiuolo* (Oxford–New York: Phaidon, 1978), but they are somewhat obscured by the many limitations of the book (fiercely underscored by John Pope-Hennessy's review in *The New York Review of Books*, 8 March 1979; now in J. Pope-Hennessy, *On Artists and Art Historians*, edited by W. Kaiser and M. Mellon, Florence: L. S. Olschki, 1994, pp. 80–86); the book's failings range from numerous objective inaccuracies (whereabouts, dates, inscriptions) to excessive doubts on the authenticity of some works, whereby he considers false the terra-cotta bust in the Bargello, the *Saint Michael* in the Museo Bardini and the shield with *Milon* in the Louvre. A similar excess of caution leads the author to bypass the topics on which his ideas are unclear, above all the famous profile portraits, which do not even appear in the book. In the same way, the worthy intention to reassess Piero's role clashes with the self-defeating comment that "to distinguish between the Pollaiuolo brothers' hands is therefore a

hazardous, perhaps an impossible undertaking". Shortly afterward, Longhi's conjectures on the connections between Domenico Veneziano and the Pollaiuolo were developed by Alessandro Angelini in the article "Considerazioni sull'attività giovanile di Antonio Pollaiolo 'horafo' e 'maestro di disegno'" (*Prospettiva*, 44, 1986, pp. 16–26), in which he stresses parallels between the altarpiece of Santa Lucia de' Magnoli and the Staggia *Magdalene*, and in the privately owned *Crucifixion*, a painting whose importance is recognised here. At the same time Angelini confidently indicates among the principal sources of the Pollaiuolesque language the drawings by Maso Finiguerra, which form one of the most significant nuclei of the exhibition at the Uffizi entitled 'Disegni italiani del tempo di Donatello', curated by the Angelini (Florence: L. S. Olschki, 1986, pp. 72–125). Instead the other extremity of Antonio's career is the subject of the noteworthy thesis by E. M. Frank, *Pollaiuolo Studies*, Ph.D., New York: 1988, arranged in three chapters, respectively devoted to the embroidered paraments of San Giovanni, the tomb of Innocent VIII, and the Roman chapter of Antonio's life (1484–98).

A new perspective is given to the studies with the long essay by L. Fusco, "The Use of Sculptural Models by Painters", *Art Bulletin*, LXIV, 1982, pp. 175–94, that tackles the problem of the working processes (the use of sculptural models by painters), and paves the way for further in-depth studies developed particularly in Anglo-Saxon countries [Britain and the United States] over the last decades. Adding to the Pollaiuolo bibliography is a dense series of contributions by Alison Wright, which associate the study of commissions, history of culture and the social role of the artist: among others *Piero de' Medici and the Pollaiuolo*, in *Piero de' Medici "il Gottoso" (1416-1469). Kunst im Dienste der Mediceer*, edited by A. Beyer and B. Boucher, Berlin: Akademie, 1993, pp. 129–49, and "Antonio Pollaiuolo, 'maestro di disegno'", in *Florentine Drawing at the Time of Lorenzo the Magnificent*, proceedings of the seminar in Florence (1992), edited by E. Cropper (*Villa Spelman Colloquia*, 4, Bologna: Nuova Alfa, 1994, pp. 131–46). Wright himself was one of the curators of the London exhibition on Florentine art five years ago, essentially didactic in style, in which the two Pollaiuolo (but mainly Antonio) played a considerable role (*Renaissance Florence. The Art of the 1470's*, exhibition catalogue edited by P. Lee Rubin and A. Wright, London: National Gallery, 1999).

In Italy it is worthwhile pointing to the clear, well-informed little book by N. Pons, *I Pollaiolo* (Florence: Octavo, 1994), offering a credible point of view of the situation, though limited to the two brothers' pictorial production, with a special focus on interpretation of the documents. On the other hand the splendid illustrations are the sole merit of the hasty compilation by F. Poletti, *Antonio e Piero del Pollaiolo*, Cinisello Balsamo (Milan): Silvana, 2001. On the awkward question of distinguishing the brothers' roles, besides the revealing studies of Doris Carl, "Zur Goldschmiedefamilie", op. cit., pp. 138, 152 note 78; and by Miklós Boskovits, "Studi sul ritratto fiorentino quattrocentesco. II", *Arte Cristiana*, LXXXV, 781, 1997, pp. 335–42, p. 339 (and, more at length, Idem, in M. Boskovits and D. A. Brown, *National Gallery of Art, Washington. Italian paintings of the Fifteenth Century*, New York-Oxford: Oxford University Press, 2003, pp. 586–95), see the present author's recent article (A. Galli, "Risarcimento di Piero del Pollaiolo", *Prospettiva*, 109, 2003, pp. 27–58).

The Silver Cross [pls. 1, 2, 4]: The clearest, most encompassing treatment is to be found in Luisa Becherucci, in *Il Museo dell'Opera del Duomo*, edited by L. Becherucci and G. Brunetti, 2 vols., Milan–Venice: Electa, undated [but 1969/70], vol. II, pp. 229–36. More recent are two monographic articles by L. Bencini, "Betto di Francesco e gli smalti della croce del Battistero di Florence", *Annali della Scuola Normale Superiore di Pisa. Classe di lettere e filosofia*, s. III, XVIII, 1, 1988, pp. 175–94; Eadem, "Nuove ipotesi sulla croce d'argento del Battistero", *Mitteilungen des Kunsthistorischen Institutes in Florenz*, XLII, 1998, pp. 40–66 (the arguments of the latter are debatable).

The Staggia *Magdalene* [pl. 5]: A. Wright, "Pollaiuolo's 'Elevation of the Magdalen' Altar-piece and an Early Patron", *The Burlington Magazine*, CXXXIX, 1997, pp. 444–51 (among other things, Wright identifies the patron). For a few further indications: A. Galli, *La Maddalena di Staggia*, Certaldo: Nuova Grafica, 1998.

The Arcetri *Dancing Nudes* [fig. 2]: A. Wright, "Dancing Nudes in the Lanfredini Villa at Arcetri", in *With and Without the Medici. Studies in Tuscan Art and Patronage, 1434–1530*, edited by E. Marchand and A. Wright, Aldershot: Ashgate, 1998, pp. 47–77. The recent restoration of the piece is discussed by G. and S. Botticelli in "Il restauro delle pitture di Antonio del Pollaiolo a Villa La Gallina", *Critica d'arte*, LXVI, 18, 2003, pp. 49–59, featuring other contributions, of use only for the photographs.

Etching with the *Battle of the Ten Nudes* [pl. 6]: The possibility of a copy having passed through the Squarcione workshop can be assumed from two documents published by V. Lazzarini and A. Moschetti, "Documenti relativi alla pittura padovana del secolo XV", *Nuovo Archivio Veneto*, XV, 1908, pp. 72–190, 249–321; in particular pp. 286–87, doc. L, and pp. 295–96, doc. LXI. A clever discussion of the issue is contained in L. Armstrong Andersen, "Copies of Pollaiuolo's Battling Nudes", *The Art Quarterly*, XXXI, 1968, pp. 155–67. Among the latest referrals: G. Agosti and V. Farinella, *Michelangelo e l'arte classica*, exhibition catalogue, Florence: Cantini, 1987, pp. 23–24; A. Angelini, entry no. 2, in *Il giardino di San Marco. Maestri e compagni del giovane Michelangelo*, edited by P. Barocchi, exhibition catalogue, Cinisello Balsamo: Silvana, 1992, pp. 36–38. A highly accurate list of all the known copies and the old derivations is provided in S. R. Langdale, *Battle of the Nudes. Pollaiuolo's Renaissance Masterpiece*, exhibition catalogue, Cleveland: The Cleveland Museum of Art, 2002 (however it systematically ignores all the bibliography that is not in English).

The Tournament: There are two contemporary descriptions of young Salutati attending the tournament in Piazza Santa Croce, wearing Antonio's armour and wielding Piero's banner: *Ricordo di una giostra fatta a Florence a dì 7 febbraio 1468 sulla piazza di Santa Croce*, edited by P. Fanfani, *Il Borghini. Giornale di filologia e di lettere italiane*, II, 1864, pp. 475–83, 530–42; L. Pulci, *La Giostra*, in L. Pulci, *Opere minori*, edited by P. Orvieto, Milan: Mursia, 1986, pp. 55–120. For the documentation, refer to D. A. Covi, "Nuovi documenti per Antonio e Piero del Pollaiuolo e Antonio Rossellino", *Prospettiva*, 12, 1978, pp. 61–72.

The Bargello Bust [pl. 3]: It was recently shown in a minor exhibition at the Museo del Bargello, following restoration (*Pollaiolo e Verrocchio? Due ritratti fiorentini del Quattrocento*, exhibition catalogue, edited by M. G. Vaccari, Florence: S.P.E.S., 2001), followed immediately by another exhibition: *Earth and Fire. Italian Terracotta Sculpture from Donatello to Canova* (Houston and London) exhibition catalogue, edited by B. Boucher, New Haven–London: Yale University Press, 2001, entry no. 17, pp. 138–41.

Embroideries with the *Stories of the Baptist* [pl. 8]: The most serious treatment is the main topic in the first chapter of E. M. Frank, *Pollaiuolo Studies*, Ph.D., New York: 1988.

The Altarpiece of the Cardinal of Portugal [pl. 9]: Payment to the two Pollaiuolo, with all the documentation on the chapel, is in F. Hartt, G. Corti and C. Kennedy, *The Chapel of the Cardinal of Portugal, 1434–1459, at San Miniato in Florence*, Philadelphia: University of Pennsylvania Press, 1964. More recently: P. Nuttall, "'Feccro al Cardinale di Portogallo una tavola a olio'. Netherlandish influence in Antonio and Piero Pollaiuolo's San Miniato altarpiece", *Nederlands Kunsthistorisch Jaarboek*, 44, 1993, pp. 111–24; A. Cecchi, "The Conservation of Antonio and Piero Pollaiuolo's Altar-piece for the Cardinal of Portugal's Chapel", *The Burlington Magazine*, CXLI, 1999, pp. 81–88.

Hercules [pls. 16, 17, 19]: On the theme of Hercules, recurrent in the Pollaiuolo production, see L. D. Ettlinger, "Hercules florentinus", *Mitteilungen des Kunsthistorischen Institutes in Florenz*, XVI, 1972, 119–42; and more recently A. Wright, "The Myth of Hercules", in *Lorenzo il Magnifico e il suo mondo*, international study conference (Florence 1992), edited by G. C. Garfagnini, L. S. Olschki, Florence: 1994, pp. 323–39. On the whereabouts and original disposition of the Medici paintings, see W. A. Bulst, "Uso e trasformazione del palazzo mediceo fino ai Riccardi", in *Il palazzo Medici Riccardi di Florence*, edited by G. Cherubini and G. Fanelli, Florence: Giunti, 1990, pp. 98–129. The eventuality that Antonio's assistant in that work was his brother Silvestro, and not Piero, is raised in an eccentric but suggestive article by E. Möller, "Salvestro di Jacopo Pollaiuolo dipintore", *Old Master Drawings*, X, 1935, pp. 17–21. Another recent comment on the Berlin *Hercules* is by M. Knuth, no. 12 in *Von allen Seiten schön*, catalogue of the Berlin exhibition, edited by V. Krahn, Heidelberg: Braus, 1995, pp. 154–56 (but with an astonishing shift in attribution to Luca Signorelli).

The San Lorenzo *Crucifix* [pl. 20]: It was ascribed to Antonio by M. Lisner, "Ein Kruzifixus des Antonio del Pollaiuolo in San Lorenzo in Florenz", *Pantheon*, XXV, 1967, pp. 319–28. Interesting observations on the work on the occasion of restoration: *Metodo e scienza. Operatività e ricerca nel restauro*, Florence exhibition (1982–83) catalogue edited by U. Baldini, Florence: Sansoni, 1982, pp. 50–53, entry no. 4.

The London *Apollo and Daphne* **and** *Martyrdom of Saint Sebastian* [pl. 22, 23]: Both are in the exhibition catalogue by P. Lee Rubin and A. Wright, *Renaissance Florence...*, op. cit., no. 43, pp. 226–29; no. 88, p. 337. For the complete restitution of the two paintings to Piero, see A. Galli, "Risarcimento", op. cit., pp. 46–49.

The Baptistery silver altar: the most trustworthy interpretation of the documentation on the altar's sides is by F. Caglioti, "Benedetto da Maiano e Bernardo Cennini nel dossale argenteo del Battistero fiorentino", in *Opere e giorni. Studi su mille anni di arte europea dedicati a Max Seidel*, edited by K. Bergdolt and G. Bonsanti, Venice: Marsilio, 2001, pp. 331–48. Also useful is the thorough entry by L. Becherucci, in *Il Museo dell'Opera del Duomo*, op. cit., vol. II, pp. 224–29.

The San Gaggio cross [pl. 21]: Documentation on the work is found in E. Steingräber, "Studien zur florentiner Golschmiedekunst", I., *Mitteilungen des Kunsthistorischen Institutes in Florenz*, VII, 1955, pp. 87–92. More recent comments include M. Collareta and D. Levi, in *La croce del Pollaiolo* (*Lo specchio del Bargello*, 7), Florence: S.P.E.S., 1982; M. Collareta, "Considerazioni sulle opere", in G. Gaeta Bertelà, G. Morigi, M. Collareta, "Florence, Museo del Bargello: il restauro della croce del Pollaiolo e di tre paci", *Bollettino d'Arte*, 23, 1984, pp. 97–104; and again M. Collareta, in *Oreficeria sacra italiana. Museo Nazionale del Bargello*, edited by M. Collareta and A. Capitanio, Florence: S.P.E.S., 1990, pp. 177–83.

The San Gimignano *Coronation of the Virgin* [pl. 24]: A. Galli, "Risarcimento", op. cit., pp. 40–45 (also for the critical history).

The Berlin *Annunciation* [pl. 25] **and** *David*: S. Brink, "Die berliner "Verkündigung" und der "David" von Pollaiuolo", *Jahrbuch der berliner Museen*, XXXII, 1990, pp. 153–71.

The canvas of *Saint Antoninus Worshipping the Crucifix* [pl. 26]: It was discovered early last century by O. Giglioli, "Una pittura sconosciuta di Alesso Baldovinetti nella chiesa di San Marco", *Rassegna d'Arte*, VII, 1907, pp. 26–28. For the

attribution to Botticini, see the opinion of L. Bellosi, "Intorno ad Andrea del Castagno", *Paragone*, 211, 1967, pp. 3–18 (pp. 13–14), and E. Fahy, "Some Early Italian Pictures in the Gambier-Parry Collection", *The Burlington Magazine*, CIX, 1967, pp. 128–39 (p. 137). The passage in the chronicle by Razzi was pointed out, though without drawing conclusions, by M. Bietti Favi, "La pittura nella chiesa di San Marco", in *La chiesa e il convento di San Marco a Florence*, 2 vols., Florence: Giunti, 1989–90; vol. II (1990), pp. 213–46 (p. 239).

The Tomb of Sixtus IV [pls. 28–30]: It is still worthwhile referring to the article by L. D. Ettlinger, "Pollaiuolo's Tomb of Pope Sixtus IV", *Journal of the Warburg and Courtauld Institutes*, XVI, 1953, 239–74. For an update, see A. Galli, in *La Basilica di San Pietro in Vaticano* (*Mirabilia Italiae* series), edited by A. Pinelli, Modena: Panini, 2000, pp. 927–32.

The Tomb of Innocent VIII [pl. 31, 32; fig. 4]: Worth reading are two recent essays: E. M. Frank, "Pollaiuolo's Tomb of Innocent VIII", in *Verrocchio and Late Quattrocento Sculpture*, edited by S. Bule, A. Phipps Darr, and F. Superbi Gioffredi (seminar proceedings, 1988–89), Florence: Le lettere, 1992, pp. 321–42; B. Kusch, "Zum Grabmal Innocenz' VIII. in alt-St. Peter zu Rom", *Mitteilungen des Kunsthistorischen Institutes in Florenz*, XLI, 1997, pp. 361–76. For further precisions on the original disposition, see A. Galli, in *La Basilica di San Pietro*, op. cit., pp. 541–47.

[6] Aldo Galli (b. Parma 1967) is a researcher at the university of Trento. His main interest is 15th-century Italian painting and sculpture: he has published numerous contributions both in scientific journals and collective volumes (among others *La bottega dell'artista tra Medioevo e Rinascimento*, Milan: 1998); he equally participated in a number of exhibitions, including 'Masaccio e le origini del Rinascimento' (San Giovanni Valdarno: 2002) and 'Duccio' (Siena: 2003–4).